BEGINNERS ON STAGE

The Story of the
Stretford Children's Theatre

★★★

Beginners on Stage

★★★

BERTRAM H. HOLLAND

FABER AND FABER
24 Russell Square
London

First published in mcmlxviii
by Faber and Faber Limited
24 Russell Square London WC1
Printed in Great Britain by
Latimer Trend & Co Ltd Plymouth

To
JOYCE
in Love and Gratitude
for your Sacrifices,
Understanding
and Encouragement,
without which
there would have been no
STRETFORD CHILDREN'S THEATRE

Contents

Illustrations

Foreword

by PERCY LORD, B.SC., M.ED.
Chief Education Officer, Lancashire County Council

This is the story of an enthusiast and a pioneer; a story of dedication and devotion to an idea. It is a story of endurance, patience and faith. It is a story of hard work, frustration, and grievous disappointments. It is, however, a story with a happy ending; a story of success where in the last chapter the joy of achievement obliterates the memories of dark and cheerless times, when failure was imminent and the cause seemed to be lost.

Bertram Holland was a teacher who was interested in the Theatre. He was a teacher who did not believe that education began on the blackboard and ended in the exercise book. He realized, many years before it was fashionable to do so, that education was a service of opportunities where talent is fostered and where interests are encouraged and cultivated. His own interests in the Theatre were infectious and irresistible. Where this interest was reciprocated there was an immediate response. Where there was indifference there was a delayed response. Slowly but surely the young and the older children of Stretford began to appreciate the opportunities that were available, and they and many adult supporters have fashioned the crown which is the symbol of ultimate success.

The difficulties have been many. There was the scepticism of those who believed sincerely that success was unattainable. There was the understandable but unjustified opposition from those who regarded the idea as fanciful gimmickry.

There were too, the more immediate and more obvious difficulties of finance; of acquiring premises; of establishing committees; of placating and soothing committees; of selling tickets; of coaching the cast; of managing the stage; of repairing the roof; and above all, of sustaining the interest of those who played in front and behind the scenes, and those who cheered from the terraces.

There has been more hard work than glamour. Bertram Holland's name will never be spelt out in neon lights. The bouquets will be few, and the applause will never be overwhelming. But when the time comes there will be hundreds of children in Stretford who will look back to these years and remember. To some they will be the nostalgia of happy days now past. To others they will be still more significant. They will be the days when they were provided with the beginnings of a lifelong interest. To a select few they will be the days when they began a career.

Bertram Holland then, deserves our gratitude. He has blazed the trail, and those who read this book, and those who emulate him will be for ever grateful.

I

The Seeds are Set

I was born at one o'clock on the morning of Good Friday, 20th April 1905.

My mother used to tell me that I cried lustily. I have often thought that we cry upon entry into this world, because we are given a mysterious glimpse at the journey ahead, and we dislike what we see. It has been frequently pointed out to me that my birthday was Hitler's also. If, as the astrologers would have us believe, the stars have an influence over us, then I must thank God I was not born the same year as he was.

My birthplace was a cottage on an estate known as 'Oaklands', a little over a mile from the village of Laceby, five miles inland from Grimsby, North Lincolnshire, so I am a 'Yellowbelly' and proud of it. To the uninitiated this means that I am a Lincolnshire-born person. Such people are always called 'Yellowbellies', and are supposed to have a mark like a guinea piece on their stomachs.

'Oaklands' was owned by the Long family. It was about seventy acres in extent, and to me, always an impressionable child, it was Paradise. Here, in the most beautiful surroundings my aesthetic tastes were born, developed and expanded.

If ever I dream, I am always back at 'Oaklands', or at college. It is a pleasant thought that our dreams often take us back to where we have been happy. It is as though happiness crystallizes a three-dimensional picture in our minds, and there we can return to draw strength when the cares of the world, for the time being, become too much for us.

When I was very small, we left the cottage, and went to live in the Hall with the only member left of the family, Miss Lilian Jane Long.

My father was in charge of the outside workers, and my mother controlled the inside staff.

I was allowed to choose my own bedroom, and settled on an attic room, with a wonderful view of our magnificent walled kitchen garden, part of the ornamental garden, and the rolling wolds farmland beyond. This bedroom was my little sanctum. Surrounded by my books, with paints, crayons, stamps, birds' eggs, and all the myriad things dear to the heart of a boy, I was blissfully happy.

I was rather lonely at times. My sister was over eleven years older than I, and more like a second mother to me. We shared many things, but I dwelt most of the time in a dream world of my own.

The woods, fields, orchards, and gardens filled with magnificent plants and trees, were my kingdom. In the dell, a jungle of foreign trees and caves, which had originally been a chalk pit, I spent hours, hunting bears, chasing spies, and climbing trees on my desert island. No boy had a more wonderful playground. I never tired of exploring those fascinating surroundings.

In the greenhouses, apart from the exotic flowers, we grew grapes, peaches, nectarines and even figs. In the orchards were apples, pears, cherries, nuts and plums of the most luscious varieties. When I think of them as I munch the dry biscuits allowed on my present diet, my mouth waters.

Being a sensitive child, I revelled in the glories of the changing seasons and, absorbing natural beauty in my daily contact with it, I grew up with a deep consciousness of being completely at one with nature. Exploring, climbing and playing in the woods with my terrier Pip, I was utterly absorbed. Every day was a new adventure.

I admired my father's country skills and appreciated my mother's cooking. Always a good trencherman, from my earliest days I was nurtured on the fat of the land.

Vividly I can recall our blackberrying expeditions. Usually these came at the end of my summer holidays. Three or four of us would go out to selected spots and spend the whole day filling large baskets with blackberries of such succulence that my very soul yearns at the memory. Returning home about four o'clock in the afternoon, the berries would be handed over to Cook, who was waiting with pastry ready. Whilst we were washing and changing, the 'Bramble Cake', as we called it would be cooking. In a very short time we would be sitting down to one of the most delectable dishes that the skill of man has devised. Packed with fruit, encased in the lightest of pastry, now soaked with purple nectar, and covered with thick fresh cream, it would make anyone moan with ecstasy at the first taste.

Long's Hall, as the house was often called locally, was a typical country house, and was built in 1876. The Long family had loved culture, and there were signs of culture and good taste throughout the house. The pictures, oil and water colour, fascinated me. Certain pieces of furniture held a great attraction. The books in the library were the lodestones of my juvenile existence.

I recall, in the drawing-room, were some antique stone vases. One of them in particular drew me, a child of four, like a magnet. I always experienced a genuine thrill when I touched part of a raised pattern round the neck. In the morning-room was a dark oak desk, with grotesque faces projecting from the front of each drawer, forming the handles. You put your hand in the mouths to open the drawers. I used to say that when I grew up I would save up and buy such a desk. Fortune favoured me. I am sitting at that very desk writing these words. It is my most treasured possession.

Miss Long usually had visitors to stay the summer. Each evening after dinner, the party would gather in the large hall, which was heated from the greenhouses. They would play the gramophone. I would creep down from my bedroom in my pyjamas, my heart beating because I feared discovery. I would crouch in the shadow of a large cupboard standing

B

outside one of the bedroom doors. There I would remain, soaking in the beauty of Clara Butt's glorious voice, the vibrant clarity of Caruso's golden notes, and other stars whose names I never knew. Orchestral pieces thrilled me. It was there I became familiar with Beethoven's mighty Fifth Symphony. Among the Morceaux de Salon, I particularly liked Elgar's 'Salut d'Amour'.

Sometimes I would fall asleep. On one occasion I awoke, icy cold, crept back to my room, and found it was 4 a.m. Several of the guests had had to pass me on the way to their rooms, but had not seen the sleeping boy in the corner.

I possess many photographs of 'Oaklands', and I often nostalgically thumb them through. I visited the house in the summer of 1963, just after my mother died. The park and kitchen garden are ploughed up. The greenhouses have been turned into pig sties. The house is now a gaming club. Ichabod! Ichabod!

At five years of age I went to the village school in Laceby, known as the Stanford Charity School, so named after its founder. School, from the very start, was a pleasure to me, chiefly because it meant books and reading.

Coupled with my school life, the Church and its various activities now loomed conspicuously in my little world. At seven I was enrolled in the Church choir.

Although I was a normal boy in most ways, I had not the slightest interest in the usual games boys revel in. I found the whole idea of hitting or chasing a ball fatuous, and boring to the point of nausea. I did then, and I do now. To me, the wasted energy, both mental and physical, at football matches in England, is nothing short of a national disaster. Occasionally I would kick a ball, or brandish a bat, but I had no heart in it.

The music in church fascinated me, and I found great interest in the sonorous poetry of the Old Testament. I remember how the word 'peradventure' pleased me, and after hearing the story of Lot and the angels read in the lesson for the day, I would say it over and over to myself as I walked home after the service. The condensed purity of the Parables gave me a sensuous pleasure. Those who sneer at the Church and its services, have never been swept up into the beautiful rituals of Christmas, Passiontide, Easter, and Whitsun, as I was. These festivals were, to my young mind, pregnant with mystery, colour, beauty, and music. The solemn austerity of Good Friday, with its hymns in the minor key, thrilled me as I personally felt the 'darkness over all the land'.

The spoken word had hypnotized me ever since I could remember, and from a very early age, the written word gripped my interest, and daily increased its power over me. As long as I could get a book, I was happy. Being on my own so much at home, I quickly built up a world of fantasy as I read my stories. I peopled the woods and fields around 'Oaklands' with fawns, demons, and playmates so real, that every day was an exciting adventure.

I used to be filled with a glorious glow as I went to church on Easter morning. As I approached the village, I would hear the mad, joyous pealing of the Easter bells being rung by the united efforts of brawny country men and lads, perspiring as the scarlet sallies on the ropes slid through their horny hands.

I walked with particular pride on Easter Sunday morning because, as was customary, every stitch of clothing I wore was new, down to the handkerchief peeping out of my breast pocket.

How we chattered and examined new ties, shirts, and suits as we donned our newly starched surplices, boasting of the new coin which had been put into our pockets that morning by doting parents.

The interior of the church, and each part of the service were a delight to me. Flowers, lilies predominant, were massed in the windows, round the font and on the altar. The subtle scent of the narcissi mingled with the odour of mysteriously pungent hair-oil on the heads of my fellow choristers.

Our organist, normally staid in the choice of music,

played a joyful voluntary as the congregation filled the church to capacity. Then, as the Ringing In Bell stopped, out rolled the Processional Hymn, and our young throats throbbed like the thrushes' outside in their spring paean, to the soaring phrases as we proudly and jubilantly breasted our way down the aisle to our stalls in the choir.

The rector's surplice glistened white, due, not to the latest plus-white detergent, but to honest labour, prompted by affection and respect. As the squire stepped to the lectern, his Easter linen and buttonhole were a picture to see. As he read the lessons, I listened with rapt attention, the words having a mantramistic effect on me. Glorious days, these, filled with thrills and pure delight. How anaemic seem the surroundings today.

I began to study the piano when I was about ten. My teacher was the leading soprano in the church choir. The lessons lasted an hour, and cost ninepence. They progressed with a swing, and soon I could play simple tunes. I well remember my first was 'Nelly Bly'. This accomplishment gave me a thrill. Conceit was never consciously present. I was just exhilarated because I could do things. This great thrill of achievement remains with me to this day. I pray God it will never leave me. I do not think it will. Our young members with their zest and enthusiasm keep it in a healthy state.

My progress in school was rapid, not because I was a genius, but mainly, I am sure, because I could read well. When I was twelve, the headmaster of the village school persuaded my parents to allow me to sit for the scholarship examination for the Clee Grammar School, near Cleethorpes. Great was my jubilation when I secured third place in the list of ten scholarships offered. Scholarship boys were rather looked down upon in those days, and, although, being sensitive, I felt this, nevertheless my work here meant I increased my enjoyment of life. The door to a wider horizon was opened. Of my great good fortune in the person of my English teacher, I tell in detail in another chapter of this book.

Since I had some eight miles to cycle to school, and the return journey uphill all the way, frequently with a head-wind as well, it always seemed senseless to me that I was compelled to play games. I hated every minute of the sports periods, and furthermore was tired after my journey. It was crucifixion to me to be picked to play in my House Team.

In football I only once scored a goal, and that was against my own side. At cricket I did manage to score a few runs, but when I had to field, I suffered such boredom that it seared my very soul.

When I decided to become a teacher, I vowed I would always do my utmost to ease the agony of the artistic child. Our hidebound system of education, even in these so called enlightened days, still compels all boys to endure 'Sport' whether they enjoy it or not.

I am longing to see the time when the arts are not sneered at in school, and when a boy who prefers to paint, act, or write rather than stand shivering in misery on the touchline, being shouted at by a senseless mountain of flesh whose only achievement is that he can score goals, will be allowed to do so, and not suffer public humiliation because of his choice.

The next village travelling due west from Laceby is the small picturesque village of Irby on Humber.

When I was fourteen, the rector of this village invited me to become his organist. I was excited at the offer, and eager to accept. My own rector was consulted, and although I am sure he was not too pleased, as it meant a choirboy less in his choir, he saw how keen I was, and gave me his reluctant blessing. So, for four years I trudged in all weathers to play the organ in Irby Church. It had an 'Ivy-mantled tow'r', which always reminded me of Gray's Elegy.

I became very friendly with the Rector of Irby, the Rev. W. Brydges-Sayers, and his family. He took a great interest in my welfare and every Sunday evening, after Evensong, I was invited into the rectory for supper. Over the meal we would discuss every topic in my ever-widening thirst for knowledge. I would often stay long after midnight, and walk the two miles home, revelling in the beauty of a shimmering moonlit night, or laboriously making my way through snow-drifts, dreaming of the future.

The rector had an extensive library, and he allowed me to borrow any volume I wished. He would spend hours showing me the wonders of pond and plant life through his microscope, and those of the heavens through a fine telescope mounted in the attic. In the lounge on a large table was an orrery. Although I was not scientifically minded, these instruments, disclosing the hidden wonders of nature, gave me much food for thought.

I had one great regret. At this stage of my development when I was bursting with joyful ambitions, with schemes chasing one another through my burning brain, I had no one who could vaguely understand my thoughts, with whom I could discuss my plans. I wandered round 'Oaklands' in a feverish mental turmoil.

At any mention of my fiery dreams, I was likely to meet with one of two receptions: anger or ridicule, both torture to anyone in my state. I am still of the mind, as then, that few if any adult fully appreciates the latent potential of a spiritually inclined adolescent. They pretend they do, but it is self-deception.

Ours was an agricultural community, and in those days, the wages of the workers were disgustingly low. To offset this a little, there were perquisites. Most workers had a cottage, rent free, a garden and a pig. They were given a piglet. This they nurtured until it was a lusty size, and then they killed and salted it. This would often be the only meat the workers' families had during the whole year. Obviously this pig was a very valuable part of the family supplies. Consequently to help the workers, there had arisen a sort of insurance society in miniature, known as the Pig Club.

For a modest annual premium, the owner of the pig was covered in the event of his pig being ill. The veterinary surgeon was called in and the club paid at least part of the fee. Should the pig die, the owner received a cash payment, which, if not equal to the domestic value of the animal, was at least some compensation for the loss.

As the yearly subscription was so small, in order to keep the finances of the Pig Club in a healthy state, various functions were held in the village. Whist Drives, Dances, Socials, and, Concerts in the winter, and Garden Fêtes in the summer were popular ways of making money.

The annual Concert was the most important function of all. It was of a pretty high standard, considering most of the items were by local amateur performers. This occasion was a great leveller. Religious and political differences were temporarily forgotten and everyone co-operated to the full.

Year in, year out, the same artists appeared, offering the same numbers, and were assured of a tumultuous welcome. Dick Wilson, the local cobbler, and leading bass in the Church choir, invariably offered 'The Trumpeter', and 'Let Me Like a Soldier Fall'. We boys irreverently used to add a line to the latter song. 'For I'm as bald as a billiard ball'. He was too. A tenor specially imported for the occasion, usually rendered 'Because', 'Somewhere a Voice is Calling' and 'Take a Pair of Sparkling Eyes'.

Bill Drury, the local comic, provided the humour with 'Widdecombe Fair' and a neat song with a chorus in which we all joined. It was 'The Village Pump'. If you visited our headquarters, you would be likely to hear 'The Pump'. One of our boys sang it in our production of *Rumpelstiltskin*.

As I progressed with my music, I eventually gave monologues at the piano. Later I teamed up with a clever ventriloquist and we travelled around the district extensively. When I was fifteen I formed a concert party. There were seven of us, all teenagers, and we called ourselves 'The Gay Goblins'. This venture was short-lived. Four of the party came from Grimsby and one from Cleethorpes. As the bus service to the village was rather erratic, it was awkward for them to attend rehearsals. My zeal, even at that age, was vigorous, and in spite of obstacles, I was not daunted. My native grit has never deserted me, and all through my life, if one venture has folded up, there has always been another exciting one peeping round the corner.

All this time I was reading voraciously. My tastes were being developed in the right direction, under the sympathetic guidance of my English master.

Having passed my School Certificate Examination with five credits, I began to think seriously of my future. My father had an interview with my headmaster, one of the kindest and most understanding of gentlemen, who suggested I was suited for the teaching profession. It was left to the Head to discuss it with me.

There was no chance for me to go to a university as my father had not the means. I vividly remember the morning my father discussed it with me. Living in my dream world, I had cherished a great ambition—to go to Oxford. I was realistic enough to know this was impossible. Nevertheless I *had* dreamed, and when my father assured me that even a training college would mean sacrifice, I of course accepted the inevitable.

After my father had quietly explained the whole position, I left him and sauntered through the woods with unseeing eyes. I eventually found myself in my favourite haunt, where I used to sit dreaming by the hour. It was a rustic summer house in the woods. As a tiny boy I had named it Robinson Crusoe's Hut. Here I sat on that eventful morning, sobbing my heart out.

When I hear students today, grumbling and often mis-using their grants, I think of that morning.

My parents sacrificed a great deal for me to go to college. They did all in their power to ensure I had a good opportunity to make something of my life. I always think of their efforts on my behalf with the deepest gratitude.

When it was settled that I should become a teacher, I was very ignorant about what would actually happen. The head-master explained that he would make all the necessary arrangements with the Education Authorities. Accordingly

I found myself a Student Teacher at The Bursar Street Boys' School, in Cleethorpes. I was here for a year before I went to college. In the autumn of 1923 I went to the City of Leeds Training College. Here I spent two of the happiest years of my life.

I met new friends, new ideas, glimpsed alluring, exciting horizons. I absorbed everything as a sponge absorbs water. Although I had a worthy, happy home, I was never really homesick. Too much was happening around me. So many exhilarating and magnetic ideas were fomenting in my brain, and they kept me arrestingly alert.

The daily discussions in the Common Room—I was in Fairfax Hostel—were stimulating. Often we talked unceasingly into the night behind shaded lights, which should have been dowsed at ten-thirty.

Delighted to return home for the holidays and enjoy my home and roam round 'Oaklands' with our dogs, I was always ready to return to college and its stimulating atmosphere.

In college I was introduced to Gilbert and Sullivan. In my senior year we produced *Iolanthe*, in which I was a humble member of the chorus. I developed a love of the Savoy Operas, perfect examples of the wedding of imperishable melodies and brilliant words. My admiration has never blinded me to a very serious defect which they possess. They are utterly sexless. This robs them of a warmth which would have improved them.

We did a fair amount of play-reading. Here again I was fortunate in my English tutor. He helped and guided my steps in literature with an avuncular concern. During my senior year we presented an evening of one-act plays. I recall I played the Doctor in *Jerry Bundler's Ghost*, by W. W. Jacobs.

Apart from pantomime, and that of an inferior standard, I had up to this seen few full-length plays. When I was about twelve I was staying with friends near Sheffield. As a birthday treat they had taken me to the Lyceum to see Julia Neilson and Fred Terry in *The Scarlet Pimpernel*. However some of our callow young theatregoers may smile, I was enraptured at the experience, and for weeks I was Sir Percy Blakeney, rescuing beautiful girls in spite of the most hair-raising odds out of the hands of ferocious revolutionaries.

When I succeeded in passing my School Certificate, Miss Long arranged a theatre party. We saw the then popular comedy, *Lord Richard in the Pantry*, at the now defunct Prince of Wales Theatre in Grimsby. The star was the well-loved Connie Ediss.

I had not been in college long, when our senior students gave Barrie's *The Admirable Crichton*. I vividly recall my bitter disappointment at the end of the play. It went very much against my idea of fair play. To see Crichton allowed to slip back to below stairs, after his efficient handling of everyone on the island, galled me. I had still to learn that the endings in the drama of life are not all happy ones.

I left college in the summer of 1925, after taking my Finals. When I thought of what the results might easily be I suffered, not butterflies, but elephants in my stomach.

At this time, posts in the educational world were scarce. I had the idea that I must get to London. I felt it was the hub of the world and I wanted to be there. Several of us had the same idea.

We applied all over the country. To get a post was our first aim. Having got one, we could look around, and change to a more congenial area later.

My first offer came from Salford. All I knew about this place was that it was in Lancashire. There were cotton mills there and many of the people wore clogs. In the autumn of 1925 I started as an assistant teacher on the staff of St. Bartholomew's Church of England School, Tatton Street, Salford, and lodged in Old Trafford, Manchester. My salary was £180 per annum.

I soon found, that, although I was in the midst of Blake's 'satanic mills', and compared to 'Oaklands' it was hell, the youngsters I taught were fascinating human beings, even if a little grubby.

My first class consisted of fifty-nine little devils. I soon had them play-reading and presenting classroom plays. Literature lessons were unadulterated joy. Some of the roughest of them had real natural talent.

My playgoing now started in real earnest. The first Wednesday I was in Manchester, I went to the Palace Theatre to see Matheson Lang in Rafael Sabitini's *The Tyrant*.

A fellow lodger was a journalist, and he frequently reviewed the professional theatre. He took me to the old Prince's Theatre. The first show I saw with him was a production of Shaw's *Man and Superman* by that very fine company, The Macdona Players. I was enthralled. Esmé Percy took the part of John Tanner. They played the full show, including the Don Juan in Hell scene.

Meeting other teachers interested in the theatre, I began to visit shows, both amateur and professional. I went to schools where plays were being presented. I was horrified at the appalling standard generally offered. I could not understand why heads and staffs were so smugly satisfied. Knowing what we had done in our own little way in my own school, I was confident that youngsters could reach a much higher standard.

I was taken to see an amateur production of *The Mikado*. This show was well done and both story and tunes charmed me. I got a score and libretto, and after studying them came to the conclusion, with my accustomed enthusiasm, that with careful rehearsal, this show could be successfully produced by teenagers. When I mentioned this to my colleagues, I was ridiculed and called insane.

All this time I was devouring books, plays and poetry. I was glutted with good reading.

In 1926 I became resident supervisor at Henshaw's Blind School in Old Trafford. Here I became acquainted with a different kind of youngster. To them, stories and music were of paramount importance. I used to read to them by the hour, and play records. We discussed their attitude to life.

Handicapped as they were, I was amazed at their happy natures. I took groups of children from my school to entertain them with short plays. They were thrilled, and so was I. In the meantime, I had met Joyce. She was a gifted pianist, and a lover of literature, as well as being attractive, and with a warm and lively personality. I was fully aware of my good fortune. There was never any doubt in my mind from the moment I met her and I was conceited enough to think too that she also had no doubts. We were engaged, and all my enthusiasms were multiplied a thousandfold.

We had little or no wealth as the world counts such things. We were deeply in love, and bubbling over with the confidence of youth and the arrogance of optimistic natures. We decided that as soon as I could get a post in one of the new type of school then being built, we would be married. I had noticed such a school being erected in Old Trafford, and wondered if I had any chance of getting on the staff.

Once more providence was kind. This school was opened in January 1930 and in March of that year I saw in the *Manchester Guardian* a notice advertising the post of English and Music specialist in that very school. Specialist posts were just coming into being. I applied, was successful, and started my duties on April 1st. I am still on the staff of that school, now Head of the English Department.

I was now in the position to do more serious drama. Each Christmas we put on a show. Our reputation as a school where drama was tackled in a serious manner grew. We certainly produced shows of a very satisfactory standard. I wrote one or two short plays which we produced with keen enjoyment. All the time I was gaining very valuable experience, and the idea of a real children's theatre developed more clearly.

Then came the war. Even that catastrophic event did not seriously interfere with my dramatic activities. It certainly closed down the Stretford Teachers' Amateur Dramatic Society. We had got nicely into our stride. I had produced an evening of one-act plays, a comedy called, *Dying to Live*, and a strong thriller *Suspect*. Now with depleted membership, blackouts, and all the difficulties of rationing, we decided to fold up, at least for the duration.

After the Manchester blitz of December 1941, we had to share our school buildings with a girls' school. Their building was being used as a Red Cross Centre, so we accommodated them in one half of our school. Though we were somewhat crowded, the experiment worked well. Each school retained its own individuality, yet at the same time we shared many activities.

Both head teachers were enlightened people, and were fully alive to the value of dramatic work. We gave several dramatic entertainments of high standard to the public.

Early in the war, a professional repertory company, The Maxwell Colborne–David Erskine Company, took over the Garrick Playhouse in Altrincham, where I live. I became actively interested in this company. For a considerable time I was chairman of the First Nighters' Club held in the lounge of the theatre every Sunday evening. My wife was employed in the box office and was deputy pianist. When I could manage it I took part in their productions.

Among the professionals I met at this time, and with whom I became friendly, was Mr Maurice Browne, of *Journey's End* fame. His friendship was a great beneficial influence. His marvellous intelligence and personal philosophy deeply impressed me. I discussed at length with him my plans for a children's theatre. Instead of the usual 'You can't do it', I received enthusiastic encouragement and many valuable tips.

My dream had developed into one of a centre where youngsters who were interested in drama and all that goes with it, could come along and revel in creative work—read, act, paint scenery, design and make costumes, and do all the things we have done during the last twenty-one years, often under difficulties.

Well, there I was in 1945, with no support, but burning with a firm determination to do something about it. But what? I felt completely frustrated. All my friends were being very kind, but offering no practical assistance. They began to avoid me when they saw me coming, as they knew that within seconds I would be battering them with my plans.

The pioneer is often submerged under the reasoned arguments of the so-called practical man, but it is only a fool who looks upon him as a fool. Once again in my life, I had usually one of two receptions whenever I rode my hobbyhorse. My listeners, often teachers, became furiously angry or roared with laughter. Both of these answers to my pleas were bitter to a sensitive person.

The idea having taken firm root, I set to work to canvass opinion and practical help. I could not conduct this plan on my own. Remember, I was a 'Yellowbelly'. Grim determination in the face of opposition is one of the main traits of the Lincolnshire native.

I recall visiting the only councillor I knew personally to discuss my plans. He was kind but pessimistic. In his view, the idea was good, but impractical.

I spoke to some head teachers in the borough. The reaction was the same. I begged them to come in on the ground floor, because to give up the idea never entered my head. Vacillating, ineffective, even antagonistic, they always finished the discussion with the same question. 'Where is the money coming from?'

I would not wish to convey the impression that I consider myself a wonderful person. I was, and still am, a stubborn enthusiast. I am sure these head teachers thought I was an insufferable bounder. How dare I ruffle the smooth mill-pond of their suburban existence!

So, for the moment I was bloodied but certainly unbowed.

2

The Theatre is Founded

Looking back on those frustrating times, I suppose I could easily have capitulated. Quite honestly I never entertained the idea. I certainly felt depressed, and sat by the hour pondering on many and varied methods of enlisting support. Then, as ever since, I had the perfect person by my side to encourage me, my wife Joyce. As keen on theatre as I was myself and a talented pianist with much experience of professional theatre, she thoroughly understood and appreciated my aspirations.

In 1937 we had a stillborn daughter. This poignant personal tragedy brought us nearer together. Possibly our greatest possession was a great sense of humour. In and out of hospital, and often in great pain, my wife never lost her rippling sense of fun. If ever I came home somewhat down in the mouth, and bitter at the frustration I was having to endure, Joyce always had an apposite quip. We would have a good laugh, and all my doubts would disappear. I would set out for the theatre with renewed strength to continue the struggle.

From my earliest teaching days, I lectured in Evening Schools, Church Clubs, Literary Societies, and Amateur Dramatic Societies, on Literature, Drama and Craftwork. During the war I had many pleasant evenings with RAF personnel on Balloon Sites around Manchester.

One evening in early April, 1945, I was busy at my desk when I received a phone call. A rather brusque voice inquired if I were Mr Bert Holland, and on receiving confirmation of my identity, the speaker said in a rather hectoring tone,

'You are lecturing to us at the Old Trafford Discussion Group in a fortnight's time.'

Now a 'Yellowbelly' is in the main a decent fellow. He will be very helpful if he is asked nicely, but try to coerce him, and he sticks both heels firmly in the ground, and an earthquake would never budge him. My ire was roused, and I replied somewhat crisply, I must admit, 'Really. This is the first I've heard of it.'

'I know,' said the voice, 'I'm telling you.'

'Well,' I said, 'I am not so sure that I am. Anyway, what do you wish me to talk about?'

'Oh,' came the answer, 'That is all arranged. You are lecturing on "The Council and Cultural Development." '

An icy hand descended on me. All my anger melted away. Here was my opportunity coming out of the blue. With a catch in my throat as I tried to hide my suppressed excitement, I gasped, 'Right, I agree, I'll be there.'

Accordingly on the 26th of April 1945, I arrived at the Old Trafford Public Library, armed with all my arguments to try to convince whoever was there, that a children's theatre was a practical possibility, and a 'Must' on any future schedule of cultural activity in the Borough of Stretford.

About thirty people were present. The chairman—the owner of the voice on my phone—turned out to be a certain Mr Moir, a Canadian. He had enormous energy and soon the meeting was going with a swing. I launched out with all the vigour of a blind enthusiast, using the subject of my lecture as a peg for all my arguments.

My talk was well received. At the end there was the usual vote of thanks, and murmured appreciation. The chairman then said he thought my ideas were worthy of serious consideration. There were one or two councillors present and the chairman suggested that a practical step be taken immediately. He proposed that any person present who agreed should stay and discuss the matter. Seven people remained behind, and after about a quarter of an hour, a committee was formed with myself as Chairman and Director of Productions. The Stretford Children's Theatre was founded.

It is interesting to note that of that original committee two are still on the Executive Committee, namely, Miss B. Williams, our present business manager, and myself.

I went home that night slightly bemused. We were seven people, with not a cent behind us, no official meeting place and a very hazy idea as to what we had really committed ourselves. Nevertheless we had faith, above all, and zeal.

Before we had had time to breathe, the snags began to appear out of the mist. Within days I was interviewed by the local press. I carefully explained my plans, and a full report was duly in the paper at the weekend. One or two national papers also reported the outline of my scheme. Much curious interest was aroused and there was no attempt to disguise the shaking heads.

Feeling a little stronger now the theatre was actually established, I again went on my heavy round of head teachers. The result was, if anything, even more frosty. Each was obviously awaiting the reactions of the others. Not one was prepared to take the initiative.

What sheep we are! Why do we hesitate, when we know in our hearts that something is sound, to put forward a helping hand and help it along? Just because someone in rather an important executive position is lukewarm surely does not mean that we should stand aloof. Are we not free agents? Is it wrong to have the courage of our own convictions? This weak-kneed, indecisive attitude has always nauseated me.

One incident in those early days is etched in my memory. I was stopped on my way to school one morning by a bustling cheery-faced little man, wearing a boiler suit and cloth cap. He said he had heard of my scheme, and wished me luck. He added that he could not help us with money, but he was a bricklayer, and if he was still alive and fit when we got enough money to build our theatre, he would willingly come along and lay bricks. He was a complete stranger to me

C

and I was deeply moved by this genuine offer. Would that we could have had such co-operation from all quarters.

I had in my mind certain plays which I wanted to produce. Realizing that I should require some older girls, I arranged an interview with the then headmistress of the Girls' High School. I had thought that as well as shows given by members of the theatre, various schools would be willing to present plays which they had produced in their own schools for the parents. To my mind such shows would provide a fine example of the sort of living drama which was being presented within the borough.

I expounded these ideas to the headmistress, and asked her if she would be willing to co-operate, first by choosing a few of her girls who could help us and further by allowing her girls to put on a public performance of something they had done in school. She listened very courteously, and then said she could not see that they could help us in any way. I pointed out that there was another way by which I could enlist members, but I preferred co-operation. She asked me what I meant. I explained that I was determined to get the Theatre established, and if I could not get co-operation, then I should have no alternative but to enlist the help of the press. I intended to put a notice in the paper, asking for applications for membership, and await results. She merely said she admired my enthusiasm, and with that I had to be satisfied.

My requests in other quarters being met in the same manner, I sent a notice to the papers, and amid a shoal of applications, the first six were from High-school girls.

I then wrote to their headmistress and told her what had happened. I said I felt justified in making arrangements between the girls, their parents and myself.

I must admit I felt bitterly disappointed and not a little perturbed. For fifteen years I had taught in the borough, and well I understood that persistence with a scheme which had not the support of the majority could have serious consequences.

Indignation at my nerve in proposing the Theatre at all was being evinced in certain quarters. Jealousy is a very powerful emotion, stronger than the largest generating station in existence. I felt now, anyway, I had burnt my boats. Had I given in under these first rebuffs, I would for ever have despised myself.

During these months when these comings and goings were taking place, dozens of young people were contacting me and flooding me with eager requests to be doing something. This enthusiasm was so uplifting after the apathy and antagonism of the adults.

I do not wish to imply that no teachers were interested, but fear of what heads might say kept many younger teachers from coming forward to give active support.

My own headmaster was most sympathetic. He was the secretary of the local branch of the National Union of Teachers. When I was considering ways and means of letting more teachers know the details of my venture, he suggested that I should address the next quarterly meeting of the Union, where most of the schools in Stretford would be represented. This I did, and asked any interested teacher to contact me if willing to help in any capacity.

I waited. Not a solitary ring on the phone, no letter, no personal approach. There was no response whatever.

Our little committee continued to hold its meetings. Some of the members began to waver. The secretary resigned.

I was fully aware that this venture was not going to be an easy job. A friend of mine in London, a man much older than I in both years and experience, rang me up to wish me luck. His experience prompted him to give me some crumbs of advice. He said, 'You will be up against it. Never mind. Don't give in.'

I have never been one to throw up the sponge easily, or shirk a challenge. Constantly encouraged by my wife I set to work with a still grimmer determination to ensure we would not fail.

The members of the Executive Committee were totally

inexperienced in theatre. This they openly acknowledged, but expressed their willingness to learn. I felt this was the right spirit and began to plan a concrete plan of action.

I had been to see the chairman of the Stretford Education Committee, Lady Robinson, and had asked her if she would be willing to be our first patron. This she had willingly agreed.

On my return from a Lakeland holiday in the summer of 1945, when resting on the top of Great Gable after a strenuous climb, I had sat formulating plans, I found a letter from the BBC. It was to say that they had heard of my scheme, and were of the opinion that it merited some notice on the air. They suggested a short talk on the Home Service Programme, from the Manchester studio. I went to see them and the result was that I broadcast on 9th November in the *North Countryman* programme.

As I left the studio, Miss Norma Wilson, who had announced the programme, asked me if I could spare a minute for a chat. We adjourned to the canteen, where over a cup of coffee she asked me many questions about my plans. She was most interested, and gave me some valuable advice. She said that if we wanted the scheme to be a success, we would have to advertise ourselves. She pointed out that if we did not let people know what we were doing, we would be completely swamped in the rat race.

I saw fully the strength of her argument, but I have a very independent spirit. It was my aim to do some work of a high standard, and let the world see that our claims were sound. In other words I wished to prove our worth.

It was a foggy Manchester night, and as I crossed Piccadilly, the isolation of our position struck me forcibly, making the chill of the fog more intense.

Here we were well and truly launched, with no money, no home, and a wall of opposition to face.

3

Our First Show

We now began to think seriously about our first production. Apart from the boys in my school and the girls from one other, I was unaware what other schools could offer, assuming they would co-operate at all. Although I am an optimist, I felt from the evidence that I would get little help from local schools. The chill wind blowing from the studies of many head teachers was apt to either reduce the temperature of the enthusiast or send up his blood pressure. In my case it was the latter.

Our major problem was rehearsal facilities. I contacted Lady Robinson, our patron and also chairman of the Education Committee. I stated our requirements clearly and asked permission to use any school in the borough, provided head teachers and caretakers agreed. The latter were very important on such occasions. The permission was graciously given, but subsequent events lacked grace.

I had certain plans in my mind and it was my earnest desire to offend no one. Like the man in the fable, I found this an impossibility. If I was to continue with my scheme, I would have to ignore opposition. I was anxious that this first venture should fully represent my aspirations. I wanted as many schools as possible to participate, and wished to employ all who wanted to help.

Accordingly I visualized a show with a large cast. Having to deal with varied youngsters for the first time, I felt a revue-type entertainment would be best. Each item would be a unit and could be given by a group from one school. It could easily be an item they had done before and the difficulty of working with strangers would thus be minimized. Talented groups or individuals could be easily accommodated.

We sent out a circular to schools explaining I was about to cast for our first show. I asked that all children who wished to be considered for a part should contact me giving their dates of birth, schools they attended and particulars of any shows they had been in, and what aspect of theatre work attracted them. I already had a number of letters, but true to childlike exuberance, many contained no addresses. I asked head teachers if they would kindly announce my requirements at Assembly. A few heads did this. More ignored my request. Some, because they thought that participation in our Theatre might interfere with their own productions, tried to dissuade their pupils from joining.

Candidly this annoyed me. At no time would I encourage a youngster to put anything before his own school. My intention has always been that the Theatre should help schools to develop their own drama. Those schools that have co-operated with us would bear witness in our favour on this point. I consider my rule concerning school performances is clear and just. It is as follows.

If one of our members is cast in a school play, then rehearsals and playing dates are his first consideration. I avoid casting him in our production, unless it can be done without interfering with the school production. If I cast someone in our play, and after we have started rehearsals he drops my show for any other, then he is not allowed to participate in another of our productions. There need be no trouble about divided loyalties if a long-term view is taken. Should a member want a part in my production and one at school, and we find production dates are awkward, I am always willing to discuss the situation. The final decision, which I expect him to honour, is left to him to decide.

I asked head teachers to offer an item in the names of their schools. One secondary boys' school offered the old favourite *The Dear Departed*. There were a few half-hearted suggestions from individuals. That was all. By the time of the scheduled audition I had dozens of names, but little knowledge of potentialities. The press helped by publishing particulars of the audition. Gradually the shape of the show emerged.

My school provided a marionette item. A woman teacher agreed to prepare a tap number. The highbrow will shudder, but I maintain the revue has its place in our work.

The producer of the play at one point evinced a puzzling reluctance to co-operate. Since I cannot endure a hole and corner attitude, I asked him what was biting him. With hesitation he explained he did not relish the idea of another producer interfering with his play. When I assured him I only wanted to time it and make sure the standard was fit for public presentation, he was mollified.

I planned to audition in a school centrally placed in the borough. Discussion took place with the head and the caretaker. Every difficulty was placed in my way. Conditions were stated which made the whole idea impossible. My own head then offered our school hall. My reluctance to use this was because the school was situated at the farthest end of the borough. If we used this venue, many children would have a long bus journey. After considering, I decided this disadvantage as compared with being at the first school. Here I would be at home; there, in a foreign land. So we used our hall.

The evening arrived. I had expected a fair number, but not the crowd which came There were children—and parents—of every size, shape and colour. I recalled Noel Coward's account of his first rehearsal of *Cavalcade*, when he had looked at the crowd of characters and felt he did not know where to begin. That was just my reaction, yet at the back of my bewilderment was a pulsating ecstasy. Here we were actually beginning. In my harassed state, as I questioned and listened, I detected a note of joy.

A few days before I had been browsing round a music shop and had found an old-fashioned action song called *The Coffee Stall*. It was a spirited little number with a catchy chorus. I bought it and planned our show around this song.

It took two or three meetings to sort out my cast of sixty. My qualms about rehearsal attendance, remembering the situation of the school, proved unfounded. Few members were poor attenders, disregarding bad weather and darkness with a geniality which was enchanting. My spirits rose. Then rumblings of disapproval began and queries started to roll in.

Are you rehearsing during school hours? What about homework? How do you pick your cast? Is it a fair method? And how about this question in the twentieth century—do you think it quite nice for boys and girls to rehearse together?

Another big hurdle loomed. Our chairman was a militant socialist. His house, where we held our committee meetings, was the Labour Committee Rooms for the Council Elections. One gentleman withdrew his daughter from the cast when we were well in rehearsal because he said he was not allowing his child to be indoctrinated with Socialism. I assured him politics were never mentioned to the children. He was angry and adamant finishing the conversation with, 'If I had my way, you would not be allowed to teach in the borough'. Tolerance! Understanding! We are still in the Dark Ages. I assured him I had got politics out of my system years before. His door was banged in my face.

Shortly his daughter met me in the street. Sobbing, she told me she did not want to leave the Theatre. I was deeply moved but helpless. My hands were well and truly tied.

I felt weary sometimes during those early days. But my wife's encouragement and the sparkling eyes and rapt attention of my youngsters at rehearsals made me feel I *must* keep faith with them. Here and there in rehearsal would be a flash of genius. I felt those tiny sparks just had to be given the opportunity of expression. No effort must be spared.

Our Education Committee had allowed us two schools for our show. One was my own school, the other was at the opposite end of the borough. We decided to give two performances at each school. Apart from one or two small mistakes all went well. We invited all the Education Committee and most of them came. Quite naturally, they were curious to see if my claims were justified.

I was delighted with the result. We had fairly good houses, and audiences enjoyed it. Whilst I was not ashamed of the product, I was not satisfied. I know our standards today are a thousandfold better. That is as it should be. No organization, no one, stands still. Progress or deterioration occurs. We have always tried to ensure true progress.

The Education Committee made no charge for the schools. We played to curtains. The few costumes required were made by parents. Props and small pieces of scenery were made in the cellar of a committee member. Teenage girls sold programmes and acted as stewards. The press praised our efforts, and the general attitude was, 'When are you doing another show?'

Our balance sheet showed a profit of over fifty pounds. We have never reached that profit figure since. As the standard of production has improved, expenses have increased.

After the curtain fell on the last evening, we held a rush meeting. We were tired, dusty, but very happy. As I had talked to parents and children in the audience, I had heard several children express their enjoyment and their intention of joining the Theatre.

A few days after the show we received a letter of congratulations from the Education Committee. We felt full of optimism. At our lowest estimate, our teething troubles were behind us. I had proved my main point. The course ahead looked a little bleak, but our spirits were high and we were girded for the fray.

4

Aims

It is my firm, unyielding belief, that our education system, to be truly successful, must be a liberal one, and this in the widest concept. All thorough educationists would agree with this view but, the world being in a frenzied transitional era, it has become battered out of all recognition.

Education as it is administered today is training our youth to have cold mathematical minds, devoid of warmth and understanding. Loyalty, decency and integrity are, in the opinion of many people in high office, outmoded, and a sign of weakness. They would never admit to this if challenged but one has only to hear students from any university talking in their relaxed moments to realize that a dispassionate, clinical, negative spirit walks abroad today. In this direction lie Belsen and the police state.

It is because I have always felt passionately that this attitude is evil, and destructive of all the nobility of the human mind, that I have ever done my utmost to foster the arts, with their powerful humanizing influence. We must train our youngsters to lead a full, productive, satisfying life.

Given reasonable health, we should exult in the fact that we are experiencing a glorious, conscious existence. Everything in our orbit should be savoured to the full and the utmost enjoyment should be squeezed out of every experience, yes, even a tragic one.

So many people consider earning a living the only goal in life. No one would deny that this is a desirable and worthy aim, and one which we should not neglect, but I claim it is not the only one, nor would I admit it is the most important.

Furthermore, the way things are going, more leisure will be forced upon man. If he has not been trained to use that leisure intelligently, he will become bored. Boredom leads, particularly where adolescents are concerned, to anti-social behaviour, and more disastrous still, to deep personal unhappiness.

I have little patience with the myopic moaner who perpetually declaims that there are no decent teenagers. If this were true, the Stretford Children's Theatre would never have got off the ground.

As I was writing the above paragraph, my phone rang. It was Jane, a pretty starry-eyed thirteen-year-old, who some few weeks ago came to ask me if the junior members could form a committee to try to help the Theatre to raise money. The committee was duly formed, and they have been brewing tea and making cakes to sell at rehearsals. This has proved so successful that they have shown a healthy profit.

This afternoon, Saturday, they have been running a junk sale. For some weeks they have been collecting some of the weirdest stuff I have seen. Jane rang me to tell me that they have made nearly eight pounds.

On Thursday last at rehearsal, they raffled a basket of fruit which one of the parents had sent. Ron, one of our fifteen-year-olds, won it. Our chairman's wife had just come out of hospital, where she had been receiving treatment after being attacked in the street by a thug. Ron suggested that he took the basket of fruit round as a 'Get well' gift from them all.

Here, apart from the drama angle, is what I set out to do—to build a healthy, happy, purposeful group of youngsters who will enjoy being alive, and pass on that verve to other people. The arts have always meant so much to me, making my life full and happy, and as English teacher for nearly forty years, I have been privileged to hand on the torch to thousands of children.

Since the foundation of our Children's Theatre I have extended this crusade. Through my work in drama with young people I have had the opportunity to see the pleasure, profit and happiness which come from the participation in dramatic work, especially in the world of the adolescent. This then was the core of my dreams. First, and foremost was the desire to bring to the notice of young folk, the joy found in the acquaintance with the arts generally, and with drama in particular.

I wanted to arrange for them to see good live drama. More than that, I wished to give them the opportunity to act themselves—if they so desired—in every type of play. If they did not wish to act, then I would find them the chance to help in every department of production, administration, make-up, front of house, scenery, costumes, props, every corner where help was needed.

This work was not to be attempted in a careless, desultory manner. We would set out to reach a high, professional standard. After many years doing just this, I am still amazed at the unexpected quality of acting we manage to achieve in some of our productions.

I am frequently horrified at the way people who should know better pontificate in children's theatre. I am often told by inspectors, drama organizers and other mandarins that such and such a play is suitable for the ten-year-old or the fifteen-year-old. They give chapter and verse as to why this is so. I listen, and think that they do not understand in the slightest what a wonderful, unpredictable and glorious thing the mind of the child is, and especially that part dealing with understanding and enjoyment.

A little incident which happened in our Theatre will clearly illustrate this fascinating unpredictability of the child mind.

In 1951 we put on *The Merchant of Venice*. On the first night I noticed a little boy in the audience, sitting all on his own. He was utterly engrossed with what was happening on the stage.

The next night he was there again. As he was leaving the theatre at the end of the performance, I asked him if he had enjoyed the show.

'Oh yes!' was the reply, 'It was smashing.'

When I saw him all alone again on the third night, with mouth open and oblivious of everything, I was really intrigued. At the interval I went and had a chat with him. I asked him how old he was, and he told me he was ten. Then I inquired which scene he had enjoyed the most.

'The trial scene,' he rapped out.

To my amazement he turned up on the fourth night, so at the interval, I took him for a coffee.

I said to him, 'Last night you told me you liked the trial scene. Now I am quite sure that you can't understand much of the play. Tell me honestly what you like particularly in the trial scene.'

Like a flash came the reply.

'I like to watch the changes on Shylock's face.'

I wonder how many of the great moguls in the theatre would ever have thought a child of ten would spot that fine point, and furthermore, have derived enjoyment from it?

Another anecdote from our production of *Little Women*. The daughter of a friend of mine—a girl of nine—came to see it. About a week after the show, I happened to call to see her father, and he told me how thrilled the little girl had been with the play.

I chatted with the child, and asked her what she had enjoyed about the show. She had an amazing understanding and appreciation of the actual plot, but above all she had been thrilled with the costumes. In one scene Marmie had carried a wrist bag—a sort of dorothy bag. (An old lady of eighty-five had given us two of them.) The little girl had been so taken with this bag that she had drawn it and even tried to make one like it. I suggested she might like to come down to the headquarters one evening and look at both the bag and the dress Marmie had worn.

'Oh, please may I?' was the immediate question. I arranged the visit, and suggested to our Wardrobe Mistress that when the child came, she could be given the second bag. If some of the 'knockers' could have seen the joy on that tot's face, I think they would have changed their views regarding the value of our work.

Ever since the Theatre was founded, we have taken groups to see live theatre whenever possible. We are keen supporters of several local societies. Our notice-board usually has several bills on display, advertising shows, both amateur and professional.

I felt that the social life of our members was very important to the success of our work. In the special chapter dealing with this, the reader will see that we attach great importance to this side of the theatre.

In the very early days of the Theatre, we realized that we were severely handicapped without a headquarters of our own. To have a place we could call ours would mean a great improvement in the conception of the Theatre in the minds of the members. I used to dream of the day when we would accomplish this ambition. How we did so I explain elsewhere.

The greatest aim of all, a theatre of our own has still to be accomplished. Had we had full support from those who ought to have helped us, that dream would have been much nearer than it is. I shall never relinquish that dream.

I visualize just the sort of theatre which is in the building at the Cannon Hill Park Midlands Arts Centre in Birmingham.

We have done much which we set out to do. There is still much to accomplish. I shall never rest until there is a firm building fund in existence. If I could see that then I should feel my efforts truly crowned.

Of course I might come up on the pools, or I might find a millionaire who would have enough faith in my plans to back them. Such an eventuality is not entirely outside the bounds of possibility.

For twenty-two years we have battled against the current, and with a struggle managed to keep our heads above water. In these artistically barren days, perhaps we should consider that success indeed. But then I am never satisfied.

It is only fair to admit that there are signs that the arts

are being noticed in England. Many cities are actively planning arts centres. In Stretford, I fear, the artistic spirit is peacefully slumbering, apart from one or two pockets of activity.

We have never aimed at making the Theatre a training ground for the professional stage. It has ever been our policy to produce good plays of all kinds in an efficient way, with our young people doing everything themselves as far as possible.

We aim to develop in our members a sense of responsibility and an active approach rather than a passive one to life.

Accepting with gratitude any financial help offered, we have at the same time tried to earn all we have received by efficient effort. Looking back, I think we can feel proud of the result.

5

Our Basic Plan

From the time of our foundation, I determined that our choice of plays should be catholic. I wanted both our casts and audiences to enjoy the best of everything. We were a children's theatre, so naturally youth would be considered first in all our planning. We were out to attract young audiences—to introduce them to the thrill of live theatre. This was a worthy aim.

Most of our potential audiences would come from homes where no one ever patronized a theatre. All they would ever see would be the 'telly' or a film at the cinema. Whilst we were out to attract children, I felt we ought to make a special effort to bring in that most awkward and maligned section, the teenager. Furthermore we must not neglect the adult.

I felt that people belittled the acting ability of young folk. I knew that with training, young children and teenagers could give fine performances, judged by the highest standards. One thing I was adamant about. We were never going to play down to the children in our audiences. My experience in school had convinced me that children, because they retain some of the 'glouds of clory', and are less tainted by the evil of the world, can appreciate much that we fail to give them credit for. Often adults are subconsciously jealous of the clear perception of our young charges. It was once said, 'Except ye become as little children, ye can in nowise enter the Kingdom of Heaven.' This is also true of the kingdom of the arts.

There are people who loudly scream about the difference

between theatre for children and children's theatre. Personally I consider they cannot be separated, nor should they ever be. To me they are complementary and indivisible. Our aim must be to attract all ages into as many of our shows as possible.

We should not chop up plays into watertight compartments. There are very broad classifications, of course, which can be allowed. As a general rule, one would not take a six-year-old to see *Hamlet*. On this point, though, I am sure, had I had the opportunity to see that play when I was five, I would have been enthralled. I have heard it stated categorically that no child under the age of five should be taken to the theatre. I cannot agree with this. We sometimes have three-year-old children at our shows, and they are spellbound by what is happening on the stage. I hasten to add that I would never take a child to see a play dealing basically with violence or sadism. But we adults should not pontificate too much about what a child should or should not see. A horrifying dragon is not likely to have a serious effect on a child, unless that child is abnormal. Children love a monster in a play. There is exhilaration in apprehension of a mild nature. Common-sense should dictate over this point.

In spite of our aims, we floundered about for a year or two, and then gradually a clearer pattern emerged. For a considerable time now, we have put on three or four major productions each season. They are chosen with the following plan in view.

1. Shakespeare, or a classic
2. Fantasy
3. Musical
4. Other types i.e. straight play, thriller, nativity, passion play.

Sometimes we may exceed this number.

When we choose a play we have several considerations in mind. First, it must be a play which is worth doing. It must

D

be one of the best in its particular class. I would not waste my time, and what is more important, the time of the cast, in rehearsing and producing a poor play. With three hundred acting members, we naturally prefer plays with large casts. Our members are not too keen on one-act plays. They prefer a full-length one—something they can get their teeth in.

Shakespeare and musicals have large casts, and give new members a chance to tread the boards as chorus or extras. This is valuable to me. It whets their curiosity, helps to get rid of nerves and soon gives me evidence of potential principals.

Another important point for our consideration is the type of cast required for a particular play. We aim to use every member who wishes to act at least once every season. We cannot always manage this, but we do fairly well. We are now using more of the younger members, as we are producing small plays in the hut at the rear of the headquarters. Some of our older members are trying their hands at production, a trend which I have done my utmost to foster for years.

The cost of a production is a very serious consideration though we have never spoilt the ship for a ha'p'orth of tar. That would be a fatal mistake at any time.

I have little sympathy with those so-called drama-lovers who moan about the payment of royalties. To me this is a clear ethical issue without any argument. It would not be morally right to use another person's brain-child without making some recompense. If you decide to produce a play, you must be prepared to pay for it. If you cannot afford to pay, then you must do without the play.

To argue that there should be a concession because it is to be used in children's theatre is feeble in the extreme, and utterly unethical.

In the early days in our Theatre costuming the play was a great problem. We had to choose a play with simple costumes because we had no money. Having built up our wardrobe over the years, it is not such a headache today. We have solved much worry by adapting existing stock.

Then there is the question of scenery. From the point of ease of production, one set is ideal. But young people like change, particularly in a fantasy.

Props can be a troublesome item. They can also supply a challenge such as youngsters love. And furthermore props can be a very important part in the success of a play.

Another consideration we keep in mind when we plan our programme for the year is the GCE play. Since these plays have to be studied and they should be seen in performance and not just read, we try to include them in our programme if it is at all practical. Many of our members have, from time to time, expressed their thanks to us for putting on set plays. They have assured us that because they took part in these productions their Shakespeare questions in the GCE papers gave them no trouble. Yet constantly, stuffy anti-arts pedagogues tell us we are doing our children harm.

While we have large numbers of acting members, we naturally have to pick our ablest members to take the leads in our major productions. The availability of talent has to be considered when we are plotting the season's programme.

This is particularly important when we are choosing the musical shows. Ten years ago we were very fortunate in having a number of excellent soloists. At the moment we are low on singing talent, so we cannot manage a really good musical.

Most reputable publishing firms now deal with plays for youth theatre, and are helpful when approached for particulars. The British Children's Theatre Association publish an excellent Bibliography of plays that is a mine of information.

Children are interested in everything. Their interests are an excellent jumping-off board for the amateur playwright. Old folk-songs and legends are packed with material suitable to be turned into plays. Fairy-tales are perpetually alluring to the very young. To see a well-loved story dramatized adds thrills to a favourite and familiar theme. National and local legends are fruitful subjects, and episodes from history and literature provide subjects of rich dramatic possibilities.

All plans should be elastic. Behind our basic plan are two main considerations; those of our members and our audiences. By presenting Shakespeare and the classics we aim to attract the older teenagers and adults. The fantasies charm the younger age-groups, and the straight plays often pull in the adults. Musicals seem to have a universal appeal. But, as I have said, one cannot regiment the human aptitude for enjoyment.

This basic plan is sometimes rearranged, enlarged, or curtailed as necessity demands, but in the main we keep to the four types of plays. To have a definite policy is always an aid to efficiency.

6

The Classics

Naturally the first plays to be considered in this section are those of Shakespeare. Because Shakespeare has exerted such an enormous influence on my own personal aesthetic development, I was determined to tackle his plays. The production of these works has resulted in such rich, beneficial work within our Theatre that I have devoted a whole chapter to this topic.

The perpetual doubters frequently question the ability of youth to enjoy a classic. I assert emphatically that if the presentation and acting are good, young people do enjoy it, and ask for more. Of course, at first viewing they do not fully understand or appreciate the play. Does anyone? Because a play of real quality contains so much, it has to be seen several times to give one a chance to savour the kernel within the shell. Indeed this is true of any work of art.

When preparing a classic, every department of the Theatre throbs with creative effort. Everyone senses something special and worthy of extra effort is in embryo. That is why we have been bitterly disappointed that these offerings in particular have been spurned by our local inhabitants. I hoped grammar schools at least would support our efforts in this field, if they avoided our fantasies and musicals. One or two from outer Manchester have, but the remainder maintain a silent, aloof attitude.

One outstanding example of what can happen, is the patronage we get from Sale Grammar School for Girls. This school is in Cheshire, about five miles from the theatre. When we did *Richard III*, they sent over three hundred girls and twenty staff. The girls came unaccompanied and their behaviour was perfect. This shows what can happen under the wise guidance of an enlightened headmistress and staff. Seldom does this school send less than a hundred.

We have presented Sheridan and Goldsmith. The research necessary in the Costume, Property and Scenery Departments when we present plays of this genre is of inestimable value to all concerned. In spite of the financial losses we have sustained on these productions, I consider their presentation was justified.

Our two productions of *Julius Caesar* differed greatly, the second being infinitely better. Our experience gleaned over the years bore rich fruit. Preparations for these productions were packed with absorbing excitement. The making of armour and so on thrilled our non-acting members. Experimenting all the time, we discovered many new materials and techniques.

An interesting anecdote concerns our first production of *Julius Caesar*. It centres around the quarrel scene. The cast was immediately attracted by this scene when we read the play through—a quarrel is so human. They agreed it would have to be done with careful conviction. So that they could develop the right feeling, it was suggested that whatever else we did at rehearsal, we should finish with this scene. Accordingly, when we finished the scheduled rehearsal, before we went home, there would be a shout 'The Quarrel Scene'. The floor would be cleared, and while the rest of the cast stood or sat around, Brutus and Cassius went through their powerful scene.

It was a thrilling experience to me to see the young, eager faces watching, mouths open, immobile; to hear the audible intake of breath following an intense moment, and then to witness the warm round of applause at the end. We would then go into a huddle. Suggestions for improvement would follow. We would criticize a bit of business, suggest a better one, or repoint a phrase. Always I shall recall such occasions with happiness.

When this scene was played in the actual production, it was just about the most artistically satisfying bit of work we had ever done. The result of a communal effort, it was the perfect example of what life could be.

School for Scandal proved to be a triumph for the Wardrobe Department. Our Sir Joseph was unusually handsome. Costume, wig, and even ageing make-up enhanced his appearance. There was a great demand for autographs.

When I read Christopher Fry's *The Lady's not for Burning*, I had a keen urge to produce it. The scintillating lines were a joy to read, and I itched to start production. Members were mildly attracted. We procured copies and read it through. Everyone immediately wanted to do it. Half reluctant, the Committee agreed and it was cast the very same evening. Rehearsals went well. Lines were learnt quicker than I had anticipated. The boy taking the priest, I decided, should be Welsh. The result was that his performance was a fine cameo.

I felt in my bones it would prove a good show. The dress rehearsal went without a hitch. The set and costumes had that good look conveying an air of quality. I was thrilled. On the opening night we played to about a hundred— the usual first night audience. The discriminating few were appreciative. Our audience on the second night numbered forty-five. It was heartbreaking.

Miss Margaret Roberts, *Daily Herald* critic, was out front. She had just returned from covering the Edinburgh Festival. At the first interval she came backstage and said, 'Mr Holland, with the quality of production you are offering, you should have packed houses. What has happened to the theatre-loving public in this area, that they can allow such a company to play to forty-five people?'

I heartily concurred with her view. This was not conceit. With experience and interest in production, one is aware when a production is good. We felt this show was of a high quality. It was frustrating to have such poor support. I was heart-sick and depressed and expressed my views in blistering terms.

Next morning Miss Roberts's criticism was published. Several pressmen came to see me, and in forthright comment I explained our many difficulties. The next week, ABC Television contacted me. They wished to make my protest visual and they arranged a tele-recording for two days' time.

I had to work fast. All my helpers are voluntary. I was ignorant of their commitments for the next few days. I rang my stage manager and explained the situation. He said he would contact his staff, and phone me the next evening. He rang me at ten o'clock. The set was up. Everything was ready. It is such willing co-operation, often at personal inconvenience and even financial loss, that makes me so grateful to our members, and so angry with the public who could not care less. Give a large section of the populace a football match, and a pint of ale,—each excellent—and they want *nothing* else. Other things matter also. I struggle not to be bitter, but it is difficult.

The camera team arrived. Our cast was ready. Producer, Floor Manager and cameramen set to work about one o'clock and we finished at nine. They were grand people. I greatly admired the way they dealt with our youngsters who were naturally thrilled and worked hard to give Miss Pam Lonsdale, the Producer, the effects she wanted.

Shots were taken from the play. Another showed me surrounded by some of my flock. One of our seventeen-year-old girls, now training at Guy's Hospital, acted as interviewer. She discussed the value of the Theatre from the members' point of view. The recording finished with a reference to the abysmal lack of support we had from the public. We all went home tired, but intrigued.

A few days later a phone call informed me that the first few seconds of the sound track was faulty. This meant a retake. Back we went to the theatre the next day. For another ninety minutes we again experienced working against a stop-watch. Eventually we went out on the beam in 'ABC at

Large'. This resulted in further publicity. Attendances improved slightly, no doubt due to the television appearance.

At this point I think I was more despondent than I had ever been since the Theatre was founded. We were doing better work than we had ever done, yet getting poor support. It was bitterly frustrating. Again my Lincolnshire grit plus my wife's encouragement won the day. Soon I was immersed in further plans. As an added help a few influential friends approached me and begged me not to lose heart. This was warming, but did not fill seats in the theatre. Others who could have helped maintained a pointed silence, or with expressions of disgruntled disapproval expressed their hostility.

One interesting feature arose from the television appearance. So impressed were the personnel of ABC by the quality of our whole set-up that they asked me to take down a selection of our members to the studio to meet Mr. Penhry Jones, Religious Programmes chief. He interviewed fifteen of our youngsters. We watched rehearsals and some recording. A further interview followed. The result was that five of our members were included in *Sunday Break*. One girl took part in a complete series of an extended feature.

7

Shakespeare

Without doubt, our greatest artistic achievements have been our Shakespearean productions.

At the mention of young people acting Shakespeare, I can visualize sage theatre-lovers nodding their heads, with a condescending smile. These are the type of people who frequently voice acid criticism of our work. They, of course, have a perfect right to their opinion. I would not object to their criticism, if they came to see the shows. More often than not, they never enter the doors of our theatre.

With a sneering smirk they say, 'Well, of course, my dear, they are good I am sure. They must be, because they have had excellent notices in the papers for years. But, I ask you, a young girl playing Juliet, or Queen Margaret. It just can't be done.'

It can be done. It has been done, and done well. These dismal croakers should have seen June Ritchie playing Juliet when she was thirteen, and Gillian Callan, also thirteen, as Queen Margaret in our production of *Richard III* in the autumn of 1964. I say with all the sincerity and humility at my command that their performances were outstandingly good, judged by the severest of standards.

At the risk of being considered conceited, I state emphatically, that I have heard the mighty Shakespearean line spoken beautifully and intelligently by our teenage performers with an artistry which has found a sympathetic response shown in the rapt attention of a discriminating audience.

When we began to read and study *Richard III*, I was very

impressed by the quality of the reading, particularly by that of the girls. One new member, Gillian Callan, a girl of thirteen, was outstanding. So well did she read that I was convinced she was being coached by someone. In her reading were the cruel dignity, the hatred, the bitterness of Queen Margaret, confidently and arrestingly expressed by a teenager. I asked Gillian if her father or some friend had been helping her to study the part. She said this was not so, and on observing that I could not understand how it was that she was showing such an unusual grip of the part, she said, 'Well, you see, Mr Holland, I like it.'

There was the answer. This is the true reason why we have managed to reach such standards in our productions. We like doing what we set out to do. Our interests are aroused and under the guidance of our small band of dedicated workers our young folk, uninhibited, and as yet not too besmirched by the snarling lethargy of the age, are agog with the vitality and zest of youth. On occasion they touch the clouds, and, sometimes, I feel, they are not so very far from the star of our aim.

I would remind the doubting Thomases that the exacting roles of Ophelia, Portia, Lady Macbeth, Juliet, Cordelia, and in fact all the female parts in Shakespeare's plays were, in the original productions, taken by teenage boys. They were early teenagers too, because they had to have unbroken voices. That their performances were good we know, without doubt, because we find from contemporary records that the plays in which they performed were in great demand.

I also would remind the 'knockers' that the Elizabethan audiences were much more alive to the beauty of language, and particularly to the quivering ecstasy of the Shakespearean line than are the anaemic audiences of today. The reactions of the groundlings to poor acting and delivery would, I feel, have been somewhat drastic.

The young lads taking the female roles would have to be fully aware of the delicate nuances of Mr Shakespeare's majestic pentameters. This ability would be of paramount importance, because the simple attempt at scenery would have to be wedded to a most delicate, careful handling of the word-pictures in the script or the mental grasp of the locale where the action was supposed to be taking place would be very indistinct. Furthermore, these lads would be working with old, experienced hands like Burbage, who would demand, and get, the very finest interpretation to match their own vigorous, exhilarating sonorities.

Shakespeare was fully conscious of the use of verbal sound to stimulate the imagination to emotional experience. He does this superbly by the emotive impact of sound.

He frequently used the simple language of the people around him, leaving the precise, artificial literary English for other occasions. His medium was the speech all could understand. It was the language of the Elizabethan Age, far richer in every way than the impoverished triviality of modern usage.

To the Elizabethan, his language was too precious to throw away. Remembering this, we must pay great attention to Shakespeare's words. We must respect them. If for nothing else, to spend time and care in the preparation of a Shakespearean production on the words alone is to be enriched beyond computation.

Because I always knew that teenagers could respond to this atmosphere of beauty which is found in the works of Shakespeare, I was, from the founding of the Theatre, keen to present his plays.

I quiver with repressed indignation when I hear the superior voice of an unbeliever, and it is often someone who does not wish to believe, say, 'But a teenager cannot enjoy Shakespeare.'

Let me relate the true story of a schoolboy's passion for Shakespeare. It is the story of my own experience.

When I went to my grammar school, I was lucky to have a very fine English master. Very tall, and bespectacled, he was conspicuous because he rode to school on a very high bicycle. It was a Heath Robinson affair, and caused much amusement among the boys. He was known as 'Billy' Minns.

In my first year he quickly endeared himself to a small group in my form. We had gravitated into the same group because of our common thirst for books.

In those days, as boys still do, we took the micky out of any insipid, inefficient teacher, but there were some with whom we risked no liberties. We recognized their strength of control over us, and also, according to our individual reactions, fell under the spell of the born teacher. In a subconscious way I think we realized that the good teacher was trying to help us. Such a one was Billy. He was a great enthusiast of the arts, particularly literature. His enthusiasm quickly found an eager response from my group.

I can vividly recall the tense expectation when literature lesson came round. At that time I had just discovered Dumas and Robert Louis Stevenson, having with the scorn of youth cast off G. H. Henty, and Percy F. Westerman as 'kids' stuff'. Billy saw that our little gang was really interested in his lessons, and accordingly expanded under our admiration.

At the back of the school was a large playing field. As many of us came from a distance we stayed at school for lunch. In those days there was no canteen. Sandwiches and a thermos flask of tea or coffee, partaken in a rather dingy classroom in the winter, or out on the playing field in the summer, had to suffice for lunch.

Mr Minns used to cycle into Grimsby for lunch. He would come back early and join our literary club. We would all wander up and down the playing field, whilst he would expound on literature generally, and question us on what we were reading, apart from our set books.

No wonder I enjoyed every minute of my schooldays (apart from when I was compelled to play games) with such dedicated teachers as Billy.

He would gently, and without upsetting the tender susceptibilities of our adolescent omnipotence—little different really from that of today—show us what to look for and enjoy in our reading. Very cleverly and subtly, without it being apparent to us, he would edge us away from William le Queux, and lead us to discover the beauty of Thomas Hardy.

On one particular occasion, I can recall, he lifted the lid of Thomas Gray's treasure chest, the *Elegy* in a Country Churchyard. I still frequently murmur to myself bits of that gem, and never without a salute of gratitude to the shade of Billy Minns.

On Library Day, once a week, when we gathered in the dinner hour to change our books, he was there to supply us with a verbal 'blurb' on the books we would each enjoy. He had an uncanny awareness of the requirements of our individual slants.

How I absorbed his zestful erudition! I could never express my indebtedness to him sufficiently. I often think of him as I find myself enthusing about a book to one of my boys in school or one of the youngsters at the theatre. He handed on the torch to me. I try to believe I have succeeded in passing it on to another generation or two. In such a way a great spirit goes marching on.

One morning, when I was about fourteen, he told us that on the following Monday, we were going to start to study a Shakespearean play. It was to be *Julius Caesar*.

Faintly realizing that Shakespeare was considered the greatest English writer, but possessing no deep knowledge of the subject, I took the trouble to read a little about this genius at the week-end.

On Monday Billy gave us a masterly exposition on Shakespeare, his plays and the Elizabethan Theatre generally. That lesson was vividly impressed on my consciousness, and remains with me today.

He played on our adolescent curiosity for interesting facts like an expert organist on a five-manual instrument. He pulled out the right stops and muted the notes which would have bored us at that particular moment. These notes were duly introduced later. Shakespeare became for me, after that lesson, a pulsating personality, and not a figure on a tomb. By the end of the lesson Billy had struck the right chord.

He whetted our young appetites by reading to us—and how he could read!—Antony's funeral oration, and another speech which appealed to me more, the speech Antony makes when he returns after the assassination of Caesar and is left with the corpse. As Billy finished, on the words, 'With carrion men, groaning for burial', there was dead silence, such a silence as is occasionally heard in a theatre after a superb performance by a first-rate actor.

When the school closed that afternoon, I raced home, bolted my meal, and shut up myself in the library. I was thirsting for more of those magnetic words. I knew where there was a volume of Shakespeare; I had often dipped into it because it was profusely illustrated. I searched feverishly until I found the speeches which had so impressed me in the morning.

Lovingly and lingeringly, I read them aloud, hypnotized by their power, not fully understanding the meaning of them, but there was an awakening within myself of a sympathetic vibration to the magic of the bewitching words.

The next morning, I was up at five-thirty. It was June, and the golden light of the morning sun flooded my bedroom. I got up, hastily dressed myself, and creeping downstairs, I went out on to the large lawn which faced south. I took the volume of Shakespeare with me. Dipping into *Hamlet* and *Romeo and Juliet*, I found lines which appealed to me. I shouted them out, to the great surprise of robins, linnets and thrushes, all busily engaged on their morning hymn of praise.

I remember a few mornings later, for this occupation became my daily joy, I climbed the steps from the lawn, leading to the terrace, and, sitting on the edge of the fountain there, splashing its sparkling waters in the sun, I voiced the Mercy Speech to a listening robin, as he perched, not six inches away, head on one side, with a look of age-old wisdom in his piercing eye.

'Oh, but,' say Dismal Donald and Jealous Jemima, 'children cannot appreciate Shakespeare.' The times that has been said to me. Of course every youngster cannot understand or appreciate Shakespeare. Let us be honest. Large numbers of adults cannot. They do not even try, and, what is worse, boast about their inability to enjoy the beauty of the master.

I am old-fashioned enough to believe firmly that, as I am a teacher, it is my solemn duty to introduce my pupils to the works of our greatest writers. I know that some of them will gradually come to love and enjoy good writing and be the better for it. To say, as an excuse, as one headmistress did, that her girls these days did not find anything interesting in Shakespeare's work is, to my way of thinking, a blatant admission of complete failure, or laziness. Had I not been taught by Billy Minns, what I might have missed!

Many new entrants into the teaching profession, have little interest in literature. Revelling in a disbelief in worthy things, they quite openly sneer at the arts. To those of us who still believe in noble endeavour and a few ideals, this is heartbreaking to contemplate.

We seem to be enlisting into our ranks too many insensitive people with no sense of vocation. These people destroy by open, boorish ridicule some of the most delicate textures of the adolescent mind. This wanton destruction is as lurid and hideous as stamping on a delicate flower with hob-nailed boots. The greatest horror of all about this is, that once these gossamer threads are severed, seldom, if ever, can they be rejoined. The stupendous responsibilities of a teacher are seldom realized by the teachers themselves, and hardly ever by the layman.

This story of my development in the realms of literature is no romanticized version, but the plain, unvarnished truth. By the time I left college, my love of Shakespeare had become a ruling passion of my life, and remains so today.

Wherever else I may go on holiday, every summer I spend at least ten days in Stratford-upon-Avon. I see all the plays at the Royal Shakespeare Theatre. My year would not seem complete if I missed this visit.

I have always found that quite a fair proportion of my pupils in school, once introduced to the charm of Shakespeare, will find something to please them. Once the interest is aroused, with judicial encouragement it grows. When the interest is there, then the youngsters themselves enlarge their appreciation of the Master.

After five years of persistent requests for us to put on a Shakespearean production, I think my colleagues on the Executive Committee of the Theatre were utterly weary, and in sheer desperation, one of them said, 'For God's sake let him have his way. When he has done one, and it's turned out a flop, he will at least have had the opportunity, and we'll get some peace.'

In this spirit of pleasantry, but with qualms in the minds of the Executive Committee, we decided in 1951 to put on *A Midsummer Night's Dream*.

This was a particularly exciting time in the Theatre. Many of our well-wishers felt we were in for a fall. Joe, playing Oberon, arrived at the first rehearsal word-perfect. Asking him how it was he had mastered this script quicker than the previous pantomime, his reply was, 'Ah, you see, this flows.'

Our fourteen-year-old Puck was brilliant. He was a restless, scintillating bundle of mischief. A sufferer from asthma, he was frequently ill, and many of his rehearsals had to be taken in his bedroom. He wanted to do the part so much and I was determined he should not miss the experience, even if we had to carry him to the theatre. Brian Trueman, now a well-known television personality, played Lysander magnificently. The unanimous opinion was that the show was an unqualified success. Since then I have had no opposition from my Executive Committee. Reference to our list of productions will show that the Shakespearean production has become a 'must' every season.

Romeo and Juliet was one of our most memorable shows.

E

June Ritchie, now a well known film actress, played Juliet. Even at that age, thirteen, she thirsted for perfection. She was never satisfied. She would phone me to query some point and to recite some speech which she felt she was not understanding correctly.

Another outstanding player in that production was Mary Stanner who took the part of the Nurse. The scenes where she and June played together were a revelation.

I am frequently asked how we set about to prepare a Shakespearean production. The best way to explain I think is to take the reader step by step, from the moment when we decide to do a specific play. Once the play is chosen, all interested members are asked to procure a copy of the script. A date is fixed when we plan to read the play through. We check to see that we all have the same edition of the full script. Some editions are mercilessly and often badly cut. To begin with we like to have the full script, and if we cut at all, we decide ourselves what cuts are to be made.

I then ask those members who would be prepared to read on the arranged date to hand in their names to me. From this list, I arrange a reading cast, and about a week before the date, the cast list is put up on the notice board.

The fact that some of the readers may be new members and their capabilities unknown to me, does not perturb me. I know what many on the list can do, and if a newcomer has the pluck to attempt to read with the experienced ones, then it is an indication that he or she is keen.

Usually this first reading of the play is good, because everyone is most anxious to create a good impression.

I make a special point of having a chat with this reading cast, and explain to them that they need not feel embarrassed if they make mistakes. I remind them that everyone has to make a start. It is essential that all should be put at their ease. This helps towards a more satisfactory performance.

The main reason for this reading is that we may all, at the outset, get an idea of the plot, and at the same time I get an opportunity to explain any outstanding obscurities. Another point, I often discover new talent on this occasion.

On the evening arranged we meet at the headquarters at seven-thirty. The play is read through from beginning to end, with no breaks unless it is absolutely necessary.

As we choose the programme for the next season at the end of the current one, we generally have this reading of our Shakespeare play in about July. We can now spend some time reading the play, allowing all the interested members to take part in turn.

These readings become evenings when we discuss every aspect of the play. All archaic language can be explained, classical allusions clarified and obscurities thoroughly explored. Peculiarities of customs mentioned in the script, and details of costume are all explained. Thus in an atmosphere of pleasant inquiry, the play becomes alive, and the members can visualize the full implications of character and plot. All this is accomplished before the actual casting is mentioned.

During this time I am soaking myself in the background of the play and in the play itself. When we were preparing for *Richard III*, I read over thirty volumes dealing with the Wars of the Roses and with Richard himself. I also saw the marathon production of Shakespeare's plays dealing with this period, at Stratford-upon-Avon.

After a few weeks of this interesting approach I put on the table in the Rehearsal Room, some pieces of paper. On the top of each piece is the name of one of the characters from the play. The members are asked to put their names under the characters for which they wish to audition, numbering them in order of preference. I collect them and arrange a cast from these names for selected scenes. A date is fixed for the first audition. Any member may attend the audition, whether he is reading or not. Usually there is a large attendance at these auditions. One or two members of the Executive Committee are present.

We may have several auditions, as we are especially keen

that the best, and only the best, should appear in our Shakespearean productions.

Once the cast is settled and the various members have accepted the parts offered to them, then we can start rehearsals proper. It may be that we cast only the principals before we start rehearsals and the less important characters are left till later. In the meantime various members are asked to stand in to read these parts. Gradually, after hearing the reading, the parts are cast. When the cast is complete the real work begins.

I allow twenty-four rehearsals. The procedure from this point is as explained in the chapter on rehearsals. Our rehearsal time-table for our Shakespearean play will be as follows.

1st Rehearsal	Act 1	Read through
2nd Rehearsal	Act 1	Read through for exits and entrances
	Act 2	Read through
3rd Rehearsal	Act 1	Exits and entrances
	Act 2	Exits and entrances
	Act 3	Read through
4th Rehearsal	Act 2	Exits and entrances
	Act 4	Read through
5th Rehearsal	Act 3	Exits and entrances
	Act 5	Read through
6th Rehearsal	Act 4	Exits and Entrances
	Act 5	Exits and Entrances
7th Rehearsal	General discussion on work done
	Special explanations if required
8th Rehearsal	Act 1	No books. Main moves
9th Rehearsal	Act 1	No books. Main moves. Little business
	Act 2	No books. Main moves
10th Rehearsal	Act 1	No books. More detail
	Act 2	No books. More detail
11th Rehearsal	Act 2	No books. More detail
	Act 3	Main moves

12th Rehearsal	Act 2	No books. More detail
	Act 3	Main moves
13th Rehearsal	Act 3	No books. More detail
	Act 4	Main moves
14th Rehearsal	Act 3	More detail
	Act 4	More detail
15th Rehearsal	Act 4	More detail
	Act 5	Main moves
16th Rehearsal	Act 4	More detail
	Act 5	No books. Main moves
17th Rehearsal	Acts 1, 2, 3	
18th Rehearsal	Acts 4, 5	

19th, 20th, 21st, 22nd, 23rd, and 24th Rehearsals. Increasing detail and business. Polish. Dress Rehearsal.

In a production such as a Shakespearean one, I sometimes call a 'Dress' Rehearsal, when the cast has an opportunity to wear the costumes, and get to appreciate the 'feel' of them. It also gives the Wardrobe department a chance to make alterations and adjustments. Such an occasion is also treated as a photograph call.

When we had given the last performance of *Richard III* I was sitting in the dressing room as the boys were taking off their make-up. With a relaxing sigh, one sixteen-year-old said, 'Gosh, I feel as though I have been mentally purified! Whatever show I am in next, I cannot possibly have a better part. You can get your teeth in a Shakespeare part, and feel a better person for having done it.' Surely no finer tribute could be possibly paid to either Shakespeare, or the work we do in the theatre.

Two short anecdotes will reveal in the telling zest of our youngsters. A week before our production of *Julius Caesar*, in 1963, we were preparing for one of our last rehearsals. All the cast had assembled except the lads playing Brutus and Caesar. Sundry remarks about latecomers were wafting around among the waiting cast, when the door opened, and in walked the missing pair.

There was a gasp. Conversation stopped in mid-air. Heads turned, and mouths opened in wonder. Displaying a little embarrassment, the two boys came to me and apologized for being late. They said they had been delayed at an appointment. They had been to an exclusive hairdressing saloon, and at a cost of fifteen shillings each, paid out of their 'spends', had had their hair done in true Roman style. Such moments are precious memories to me.

When one of the lads said, 'You're not vexed, are you, Mr Holland?' I could hardly find the words to tell him how thrilled I was at their zeal. Allowing a few moments to let their friends examine the result of their keenness, and to comment on the fact that a Beatle haircut and a Roman one were very similar, we then attacked the assassination scene with added gusto.

The other story concerns *Richard III*. When we were in rehearsals for this production, one of the cast, a thirteen-year-old, managed to persuade his father to stop a night at Stratford-upon-Avon, on the way for the family holiday. Somehow he managed to get a ticket for a performance of *Richard III*. This had cost him twelve shillings and sixpence.

When he returned to the Theatre, he was full of the performance. He told me how he had enjoyed the show. As I had seen this production, we could compare notes. His grasp of the finer points of the presentation was excellent. After he had told me of his enjoyment, he took out of his pocket wallet a small piece of material like bakelite. He explained how in one scene the plotters all brought down their maces on the council table with a mighty blow to emphasize their oaths, and this splinter had flown off into his lap. Very lovingly he passed it around among the admiring cast. A certain kind of awe was present that evening, and a depth of meaning, hitherto absent from our acting, showed itself.

Some years ago a friend of our Theatre gave us a statuette of Shakespeare. He stands in our rehearsal room and has no more loyal band of worshippers than the Stretford Children's Theatre.

We have just finished a production of '*Othello*'. In passing,
I would say this has been our finest Shakespearean production to date, a truly memorable week which we shall
always remember. The following shows my first analysis of
the play.

Producer's analysis of *Othello*.

ACT 1 *485 lines*

SCENE 1 VENICE, a street
      Roderigo
      Iago
      Brabantio
      2–4 Servants (Brabantio's)
      120 lines

SCENE 2 THE SAME
      Othello
      Iago
      Cassio
      Brabantio
      3 Servants (Brabantio's)
      3 Servants (Othello's)
      4–6 Officers
      90 lines

SCENE 3 COUNCIL CHAMBER
      Duke
      First Senator
      Messenger
      Iago
      Brabantio
      Othello
      Roderigo
      Desdemona
      4 Senators

Attendants (Othello's)
Attendants (Brabantio's)
275 lines

ACT 2 *456 lines*

SCENE 1 SEAPORT IN CYPRUS Before the Castle
Montano
Four gentlemen
Desdemona
Emilia
Cassio
Iago
Roderigo
Othello
Attendants (Othello's)
Attendants (Desdemona's)
231 lines

SCENE 2 THE SAME
Herald
Sundry (To be decided later)
12 lines

SCENE 3 THE SAME
Othello
Cassio
Iago
Montano
Roderigo
Desdemona
Gentlemen
2 Attendants (Othello's)
2 Attendants (Desdemona's)
Servants
213 lines

ACT 3 *567 lines*

SCENE 1 THE SAME
  Desdemona
  Cassio
  Emilia
  Othello
  Iago
  420 lines

SCENE 2 THE SAME
  Desdemona
  Othello
  Emilia
  Cassio
  Iago
  Bianca
  147 lines

ACT 4 *428 lines*

SCENE 1 THE SAME
  Othello
  Iago
  Cassio
  Bianca
  Lodovico
  Desdemona
  Attendants (Desdemona's)
  174 lines

SCENE 2 ROOM IN THE CASTLE
  Othello
  Emilia
  Roderigo
  Iago
  Desdemona
  187 lines

SCENE 3 DESDEMONA'S BEDCHAMBER
       Desdemona
       Emilia
       67 lines

ACT 5   *377 lines*

SCENE 1 A STREET
       Iago
       Cassio
       Roderigo
       Lodovico
       Soldiers
       Gratiano
       67 lines

SCENE 2 DESDEMONA'S BEDCHAMBER
       Othello
       Desdemona
       Emilia
       Montano
       Iago
       Lodovico
       Cassio
       4 Officers
       310 lines

TOTAL *2,313 lines*

Estimated playing time 2 hours 30 minutes.
One interval. Place to be decided later.

8

Fantasy Plays

Since our main aim is to interest youth, I have searched for plays attractive to the fantastic in the child mind. I detest the person who would starve the child of fantasy. Today, too many children are robbed of childhood wonderland. If this natural yearning is unsatisfied in youth, it can later develop undesirable manifestations.

Fairy-tales loom large in this section of our work. Fortunately such plays are available. Grim, unimaginative folk frown on the idea of allowing children to indulge in fantasy. I was horrified recently to hear of a Junior headmaster who allowed no fiction in his school. How such a person has ever been allowed to teach young children is beyond comprehension. The mess we are in today is largely due to stupid people with no imagination.

Such people, in charge of young children, shudder to contemplate the idea of witches and dragons being introduced to their pupils. Their argument is that it would frighten the children. They even bar good fairies. They explain that the fairy's wand, having the power to change Cinderella's rags into a glittering dress, and the pumpkin into a golden coach, fosters the idea of something for nothing.

What a stupid, barren argument! How wicked to atrophy imagination in that way! Such people cannot have the faintest understanding of a child. I cannot visualize more unattractive adults. When shall we stop such people being allowed to mould the child mind? Did these individuals ever enjoy childhood? I think if their backgrounds were investigated frustration from birth would be evident—perhaps before.

The weird, the mildly eerie, dwarfs, goblins are attractive to youngsters. Provided children do not see sadism or violence portrayed, the antics of the dragon, whilst mildly spine-chilling, are treated as fun. Another point, fantasy plays have pleasing endings. Good is rewarded; evil punished.

In this debunking age, the verities remain. Whatever humanists or any other -ists avouch, to show youth that life is a struggle, and that to achieve anything worth-while a genuine effort must be made, is surely not an unreasonable or harmful way to train a child.

Pantomimes retain popularity up to a point. They contain music and fantasy, but are not very satisfying fare to many modern youngsters. In our early days, I arranged one or two, and they were successful. Later we did a particularly interesting *Cinderella*. I had seen this in 1945 at Southport Rep, for whom it had been specially written by V. C. Clinton-Baddeley. The attractive music was by Gavin Gordon. My wife played one of the pianos. I was determined we should do this pantomime. It was a huge success. June Ritchie played Prince Charming. Samuel French publish the libretto and loan the score.

A most rewarding musical fantasy is *The Land of the Christmas Stocking*, which we have presented twice. Our patrons agree it is an ideal show for junior audiences. Older children and adults enjoy it. The composer of the music is Mabel Buchanan. I met her and we decided to join forces and write a show. Alas, pressure of work in school, plus my theatre commitments, have meant that this idea has never materialized.

The beauty of this show is that it is completely based on well-known nursery rhymes. The plot concerns two rather naughty children, Tom and Tilly. It is Christmas Eve, and they declare they do not believe in Father Christmas. Wee Willie Winkle overhears them, and when Father Christmas arrives down the chimney, Willie tells him of the children's disbelief. Father Christmas is shocked, and decides to take the children, with their nurse, back to his kingdom and teach them a lesson. There the children meet all the nursery rhyme characters, and after some exciting adventures they come to realize that Father Christmas really exists. In the last act we see the preparations for the delivery of toys on Christmas morning. In Father Christmas's workshop sacks are being filled with toys, as he watches with an eagle eye.

In this scene, on our first night, we had groups of children filling three sacks. On each sack was the name of a district in Stretford. When the curtains opened there was a roar of laughter from the audience. Fearing that something was wrong, I slipped into the back of the theatre. I had to smile myself, at the same time making a mental note to have a word with the Property Mistress. One of the sacks—the one nearest to the audience—had been placed wrong way round. Instead of the words 'Old Trafford', 'Fison's Manure' appeared clearly.

The background of cave, mountain, castle, dungeon and palace is beloved of young folk. Any manifestation of magic, however simple, is met by riveted attention. Using such a formula, I have written two full-length fantasies which we have successfully presented. In my first one, *The Willow Pattern Dream*, I apparently provided what the audience love. Of course I was very gratified, as it had been an experiment. Much had developed during rehearsal and from discussion with the cast. The main attraction was the Emperor's favourite Pekinese dog. We used a real dog, and it just about stole the show.

The second Play, *Rumpelstiltskin and the Three Wishes*, seemed to grip the audience from the opening. I used all the touches I have mentioned: lightning, thunder, a horrid dwarf, a witch, and what proved a favourite, Rumpelstiltskin's familiar, a spider called Satan. The witch arrived on the scene via the Magic Well to the accompaniment of thunder. All these well-worn effects carried the open-mouthed audience away on the wings of fantasy. No author could wish for higher appreciation than that of a modern miss of ten years who in a gush of pleasure said, 'It was better'n than the telly.'

June Ritchie, playing in the West End as I write these words, with several films to her credit, and acclamations at the Edinburgh Festival, following a season at the Nottingham Playhouse, joined our Theatre when she was nine years of age. Her personality even at that tender age was sparkling. She had an open, generous disposition, and missed not one jot of instruction which came her way. When she was ten, she took the lead in the happy little musical *The Windmill Man*. She scintillated, a tiny star, and in that, her first performance, the whole cast was enriched by her performance.

I vividly remember the last evening of this show. I went into the dressing room after the final curtain. There I found June, sitting on her mother's knee, sobbing. 'Good gracious June,' I said, 'whatever is the matter?' With tears streaming down her cheeks, she jumped down, and flinging her arms around my neck, sobbed out, 'Oh, Mr Holland, I'm crying because it's over.'

I sat her on my knee and said, 'Now listen, June. If you will work hard, when you are fourteen, you shall play Juliet for me.' I had seen the talent there. With the quivering earnestness of youth, she gasped out, 'Oh, I *will* work, Mr Holland, I *will* work.'

She did work, and still does. Never has she dodged hard work, and the attention to detail which stamps the true artist. She is ever willing to learn. When I went into the dressing room with my notebook, after having watched an act, June's words were always, 'What can I do to improve my performance?' Too many young people today, in all walks of life want to get to the top and earn big money without hard work.

There is an interesting fact concerning our second production of *The Windmill Man*. Two characters in this show are a brother and sister. They are poor city children spending a day in the country who wander into the palace gardens. In this presentation a brother and sister did play these two characters.

A playwright who in my estimation has been able to catch the appreciation of young audiences with a series of plays based on well-known fairy tales is Nicholas Stuart Gray.

I was recently talking to a long-haired, not too clean modern who liked to think he was *avant garde*. He pooh-poohed my admiration of Gray's plays, and brought up his big guns. His main ammunition was sneering—the usual brash debunking with no idea of what he would offer in the place of these charming little plays. He vaguely suggested 'Creative Drama'. I have the greatest admiration of this kind of thing when it is done well, but I have seen so much time wasted with no real results, using this type of drama work.

We have produced five of Gray's writings, each one an undoubted success. Three of them we have presented twice. I consider Gray's *Beauty and the Beast* one of the most satisfying plays of its kind, both for young and old. The two main characters, the absent-minded magician, Hodge, and his baby dragon nephew, Mikey, are two of the most attractive characters ever conceived in children's theatre. The magic in this play is enthralling. Apart from the plot, there is a subtle undertone very attractive to adults. The eternal verities, coated with the icing of delight, lift these little dramas on to a high level without obvious moralizing.

We also enjoyed presenting *The Heartless Princess* by Franklyn Black. In some ways it is a peculiarly written play, but it proved popular. The main character, the Fox, is a loveable rogue. The witch is a nasty piece of work whose perpetual cold causes much amusement, and diminishes her efforts to appear powerful.

I cannot get out of my mind the headmaster who allows no fiction books in his school. He would provide the material for the plot of a play. I should certainly cast him as the Ogre.

I fear it would be impossible to melt his heart. Let me here plead with head teachers and English specialists in particular. Allow your children to see good plays. It will stimulate their imagination and provide them with great enjoyment.

Fantasy plays call for fantastic scenery. How our youngsters love the weird tree shapes, and unusual patterns thrown by the shadows cast by weird costumes. Eerie music faded in to add to the atmosphere all ensure that they will revel in a glorious experience. When we play these shows, I often creep down silently into the auditorium to watch the faces of the enraptured audiences and hear the exclamations made by the uninhibited youngsters, absorbed in the magic of the moment. These are some of the most exciting moments of our work. This utter involvement is a thrilling thing to witness. It often acts in a cathartic manner. When we did *The Snow Queen* I overheard a little boy take in a lungful of air audibly, following a particularly tense moment ending an act, as the house lights came up, say, 'Cor, I feel better for that!' I wonder if our non-fiction-loving head ever experienced such a moment.

9

Musicals

As I was a music lover, it was not long before we had a little music as a relaxing agent at rehearsals. We sang anything and at any odd moment, just for the fun of it. Frequently when we had finished the main rehearsing we would have ten minutes of the lastest popular song. Just when the youngsters least expected it, I would slip in a Savoy Opera record, and in no time at all, they would find they were joining in, and tapping out the rhythm.

Our first two shows contained solos and concerted numbers. In the preparation of these we discovered that many of our members had really beautiful voices.

On our 'Open' evenings, the more talented gave solos, and we soon had a few potential principals for a musical show.

When we had been in existence for about eighteen months, our secretary resigned. As the Theatre was by then on its feet, and definitely expanding, I wanted an experienced person to take on what I consider is just about the most important position in any organization. I approached a lady whom I had known for some time, Miss Mabel Bagley, and asked her if she would consider taking over the post of secretary.

Miss Bagley was an ex-Mayoress of Stretford, and personal secretary to the General Manager of what was then known as Metro-Vicks. In addition, she was a singer of some talent. She accepted the post, and there began a long period of successful co-operation with an efficient secretary as my assistant.

F

I was convinced that young people could successfully put over a Gilbert and Sullivan opera. I discussed this with Miss Bagley, who had qualms but agreed to help.

My own favourite Savoy opera was *The Mikado*. I suggested to the Executive Committee that we produced this. As with Shakespeare, they demurred. Eventually they fell before our exhortations and a date was fixed.

I learned afterwards that the popular view within the Theatre was that we had bitten off more than we could successfully digest. It was hotly expressed that I had stampeded everyone into acceptance. This attitude was actually expressed in the local press.

The chorus presented little difficulty. Girls we had in plenty, all with attractive voices. Boys were in good supply, but their age meant the quality of their voices left much to be desired. Nevertheless I was confident they would not disgrace us.

In our principals we were unusually lucky. Yum Yum had a voice out of this world. It really had an incredible quality for a girl of seventeen. Katisha, a vivacious and attractive girl of fourteen staggered us by the way she tackled this exacting role. Not only did her voice develop an amazing power and quality. but her understanding of the part was amazing. Ko Ko was a natural comic, Nanki Poo a most pleasing tenor with a personality to match. The Mikado himself had a sound singing, and an excellent speaking voice. Our Three Little Maids were captivating—especially to the boys' chorus. Rehearsals, though arduous, went well, and as the time passed and the opening night seemed to rush nearer, excitement mounted.

As all producers do, as zero hour approached, I wondered what the result would be. I realized that a great deal hung on this production. If we had a success, then our stock would soar. Should we have a failure, then it would mean the end of the Theatre. Nevertheless I pushed to the back of my mind the very whisper of failure.

The week before the show the local press began to forecast

the result. They summed up the possibilities, and came to the conclusion that there was nothing to fear. This was very gratifying, but meant that we just must *not* have a failure.

Miss Bagley worked overtime with the principals, and I wrestled with the chorus. It was a most interesting, if rather nerve-racking time.

I have often wished I had kept a detailed rehearsal time-table, as I now do. It would be interesting to know how many hours' work we put into that first Gilbert and Sullivan.

We decided to give up the idea of having an orchestra, when it proved almost impossible to enlist voluntary players. Having heard so many amateur operatic productions where poor orchestras have ruined what could have been excellent shows, I felt we were much better off with a good pianist. We were fortunate in securing the services of a really brilliant pianist, and what was so much more important, one with whom it was a pleasure to work.

On the opening night I was bathed in nervous perspiration before the curtains opened. The opening chorus was a bit reedy, but from the entrance of Nanki Poo, nothing went wrong. The Three Little Maids captivated the audience, Ko Ko had the patrons in the hollow of his hands, and enjoyment enveloped us all like a cloak. We had a full house, many there out of a sharp-edged curiosity, and when I laid down my baton, at the end of Act One, a storm of applause left no doubt in anyone's mind of their opinion.

As I ascended the steps leading to the dressing rooms, mopping my streaming brow, applause ringing in my ears and a tumultous joy in my heart, our treasurer met me with out-stretched hand. Alan was the science master on the same staff as myself. He was a very fine man, with a brilliant brain, whom I have always admired greatly. He is a true scientist. With Alan everything must have a cast-iron proof. There must be no monkey business, nor foggy flights of fancy.

Speechless for a moment, he wrung my hand and then said, 'I want to be the first to tell you what I said when I heard you were going to tackle a Gilbert and Sullivan. My remark was, "This is the end of the Stretford Children's Theatre." I want to tell you personally, I take all that back. I wish to be the first to say "Magnificent". Congratulations. I know the second act will be even better, I feel it.'

Alan will never know what those remarks meant to me and my ego coming just at that particular moment. Such experiences, pinpointed in time, remain as very precious possessions.

The second half of the show was better. The attractive number 'Here's a How D'ye Do' was encored seven times, and even then we had to start the next number in the midst of loud cheers.

I shall never forget the scene at the end of the performance. People just stood up on the seats and cheered. I felt that we had more than proved my theory that young people could put over a production in truly professional style. Furthermore, they enjoyed doing it, and were better individuals for the effort.

We did *The Mikado* again some years later. Some of the cast took the same parts as in the first production. It was a good performance, but, to me, lacked some of the sparkle of the first time. It was just a reiteration of what we had proved earlier, without its pristine glory.

The other musicals which gave us great pleasure were *The Quaker Girl* and *The Arcadians*. Both are old and worn, but full of attractive tunes. They enabled us to give large numbers of members an opportunity to tread the boards for the first time.

Our Doody in *The Arcadians*, a twelve-year-old lad, was hailed as a discovery. He stopped the show every night with his number 'I've got a Motter'. He has turned professional and now has a beat group.

When I was unable to get a certain play which I required, I went to Samuel French's. Always helpful, they recommended a musical which had just come into their hands. It was *The Land of the Christmas Stocking* that I have already described in an earlier chapter. They lent me a copy. I read it in the train, liked it and decided to put it on. The music, by Mabel Buchanan, is attractive and not complicated. The libretto is by Henry D. G. Foord. A large cast is necessary, and with colourful costumes and scenery it makes a dazzling, exciting show. We have presented this twice. Both cast and audiences have enjoyed it.

We have enjoyed all the musicals we have done, but perhaps the most exciting of them all was *Love From Judy*. This will ever remain in my memory as a special show, because it was the last time June Ritchie played for us. She gave such a superb performance that people talk of it to this day. The part of Judy might have been written for her. It brought out all her talent. She won an Oscar from the *Manchester Evening Chronicle* for her performance, and richly she deserved it. We would like to do the show again, but I hesitate. Youngsters with the talent of a June Ritchie are difficult to find.

We had little trouble casting the play. The story is attractive, and rehearsals of the spoken word went well. It was a different story with the music. In the first place, the male chorus gave us a lot of trouble. Our youngsters develop earlier today. Consequently the male teenage voice has deteriorated. Try as I might, I could get little out of my lads. Give them a Pop number, and they will sing. There were some good choruses in *Love From Judy* but I could get nowhere with them in rehearsals. All I could raise was a banshee wail.

There was a song we nicknamed the 'Banjo' Song. It was catchy, jolly, and I could visualize just how it ought to go. We could get it nowhere near my idea. I felt completely frustrated. One night after a particularly strenuous but futile rehearsal, when I was mopping my brow and feeling particularly depressed, I suggested to the surrounding chorus that it might help if we could get someone into the chorus who could play a banjo.

Sitting in the crowd was a small, dark-haired girl, one of our dancers. She piped up, 'I have a cousin who can play the banjo.' I stopped mopping and pounced. Where does he live? How old is he? An interview was arranged. He was nineteen, rather shy, but when we persuaded him to play there was no doubt of his ability. He was a wizard.

We managed to convince him, reluctant at first, that it would be fun to help us, and of the greatest assistance to us. At his first rehearsal he had us all spellbound. The chorus could not speak, let alone sing. We let him play anything. We listened. Then at the next rehearsal we started on the choruses. Words could never describe the exhilaration we felt when we started the Banjo Song. It zipped into the right idiom immediately. On the first night of the show, at the end of this song, the audience rose in a body and yelled for more.

A serious crisis arose over a pianist for this show. Our regular one had had to resign on doctor's orders. Although I tried for weeks, here we were, twenty-one days before the show, with no pianist. I had done my best during rehearsals but I was not prepared to play for the actual performance. I pleaded with various people. They all declined for a variety of reasons. I was getting really worried.

In a frantic mood I rang Tom Wildern, then critic of the *Manchester Evening Chronicle*, and now chief critic of the *Manchester Evening News*. I asked him if he could help us in our predicament. He had suggested the show to me and had always watched our development with the greatest of interest. I felt if anyone could help, he was the man. I also knew he would if it was in his power. Immediately he said he thought his wife might play for us. I straightway rang, and in five minutes it was settled. As I left the phone box, I almost swooned with relief.

Yet another ugly snag had reared its ugly head. Our leading man, Rodney Jones, could not sing a note. I think he was tone deaf. In every other way he was ideal. In appearance he was a matinée idol, with a particularly rich and attractive speaking voice, but he was unable to sing a single note.

Well, every difficulty is an opportunity. We could get away with this state of affairs, except in one song. One of the highlights of the show is the theme song, '*Love From Judy*'. In the presentation of this, Judy and Jervis each sit on opposite sides of the stage. The stage is in darkness except for a spotlight on each of them. Judy is writing a letter to Jervis, and sings her message, then the spot fades. The other spot then comes up on Jervis who has received the letter, and as he reads it, sings the words.

We overcame our difficulty by allowing Jervis to read the letter, and as he looked out over the auditorium, three girls softly sang the tune into a backstage microphone. This came off beautifully. Candidly, I thought the impact it made on the audience was an improvement on the original arrangement.

And so we had a successful show, in spite of all our difficulties, or was it largely because of them?

June's performance was superb. She tore at our heart strings, and by her boundless energy, rich, warm personality and faultless artistry, she drew every member of the cast with her. The whole production was lifted to a sphere seldom reached in the amateur stage world. It was a most exhilarating and wonderful experience for us all and remains one of the happiest memories of our theatre.

Following *Love From Judy*, we presented another musical, *A Girl Called Jo*. This was the musical version of *Little Women* and was the world amateur première. It nearly proved a failure; we only just saved it from being an utter flop. Many patrons liked it, but personally I was bitterly disappointed with it. Coming immediately after the success of *Love From Judy*, I felt it all the more keenly. The cast themselves knew it was weak. On the first night, at the end of the performance we usually have a little meeting in the dressing rooms to discuss the weak spots in the show. On the first night of this show, I was kept out front talking to one or two patrons. When I got into the dressing rooms, not one of the cast was there. They had all flown. I was not actually ashamed of the performance, but I felt it was not up to our usual standard.

I am often accused of never being satisfied. That is true, I never am. When I reach that petrifying state, it will be time someone shoots me because there would be no further development. Complete satisfaction is the refrigeration of all effort.

We have done a few other Savoy Operas; all, I think we could say, were successful productions. At the moment, as I have said, we are denuded of soloists. Fewer people seem to be interested in singing. The screaming, grunting, and moaning which are today accepted and encouraged as an example of the human voice, mean that these young people who have a decent voice, misuse it.

The quality of singing required for Gilbert and Sullivan is rarer today than it was in the early days of the Theatre. This may be a regional shortage, but I have heard the same moan from many people, when I have attended conferences in different parts of the country.

Fewer people today seem to have the staying power to spend time and effort on some of the worth-while hobbies. I consider we have been very fortunate to have kept the flag flying at our Theatre for twenty-one years.

Audience participation is more often found in musical shows than in other kinds of dramatic presentations. The occurrence of a particular popular melody means that even if there is not open singing on the part of the audience, there is a subtle mental participation. In *The Quaker Girl* for instance, the older patrons sing the well-known choruses. To be able to do that is an added attraction.

Musicals can be a headache to the stage staff, and costume and props departments. As we can usually draw on willing helpers for these sections, we are not unduly worried. My stage manager, I fear, would tell me it is not quite so easy at the present time. We are meeting a little more reluctance, compared with how it used to be.

Chorus work can often be done almost without the cast knowing they are rehearsing. We start the songs by having a record session. We pick the numbers with the most attractive melodies and rhythms. In this way, it is amazing how quickly the songs are picked up.

Timid people overrate the difficulties of a musical production. 'Well begun is half done' is the attitude to adopt.

A good pianist is essential, both for rehearsals and the show. Two pianists are better, provided they can work amicably together. This is most important. If there are two it makes the rehearsals less difficult. They can arrange a time-table so that neither is overworked.

It makes a very attractive trio if you can enlist the services of a good drummer. A small orchestra, provided they are not too amateurish, adds to the effectiveness of a production. This is a thrill I have yet to experience.

There is one point about having an orchestra in a youth theatre. It would be necessary to have it present much more often than with an adult society. The latter usually has the orchestra in for the dress rehearsal, and that is the only time the cast has the experience of singing with it before the actual show. The ideal position would be a youth orchestra under the baton of an enthusiast who would co-operate fully with the director of the theatre.

If one has patience, the part-singing in any average musical can be tackled with confidence. Outside Grand Opera, there is nothing which defies optimistic effort. Given the desire to do it and a keen cast with average talent under the eye of an energetic director, you cannot fail. The resulting production will be an exciting adventure which will richly reward all the effort expended.

10

Other Plays

In this category I include all 'straight' plays. Romantic dramas, however we argue to the contrary, are still popular. They have a special appeal to the teenager, in spite of the latter's tough façade. Romance may have a different appearance today. Basically it is the same. Realizing this we have always included romantic plays in our plans.

Because of my youthful experience I had always felt I would like to try *The Scarlet Pimpernel*. No acting edition was available, so I had to contact Miss Phyllis Neilson-Terry who controls the rights of this play. She graciously gave us permission to present it and furthermore loaned us the scripts.

Immediately we received them, we cast the play and started rehearsals. We all decided that this must be a special production. Each department of the Theatre set to work with zest. A friend of mine, a clever artist, designed us some striking sets. The Wardrobe Mistress surpassed herself. In the ballroom scene, the Prince of Wales was in midnight-blue velvet, Sir Percy in apricot satin and all the ladies were exquisitely gowned.

We decided on a lavish publicity campaign that included a personal appearance of Miss Terry. Three of the committee met her at the station, and after dinner with the Mayor and Mayoress of Stretford, Councillor Frederick Matthews, J.P., and Mrs Matthews, at the Town Hall, we went on to the theatre. Miss Terry was introduced to our Sir Percy and Lady Blakeney. She watched the performance, and at the end was introduced to the audience. We gave her an album of photographs of our principals to take to her mother,

Julia Neilson-Terry, the original Lady Blakeney. Miss Terry also paid a moving tribute to our work. We then had a buffet supper in our large dressing room, where she met the rest of the cast and signed autographs. Our youngsters were delighted and it was a memorable evening in the history of the Theatre.

Daddy Longlegs was one of our early shows. Sentimental? Yes, but wholesome. A healthy human incident that brings a lump to the throat should not be debunked. Had Hitler and his thugs had a touch of sentiment, they would never have sent millions to the gas chambers. Nor would today's hooligan hang up a dog, leaving it to die in agony, or beat up an old lady, if he could feel a qualm of conscience.

Some of our critics who applaud violence and praise the products of sick minds would not betray humanity if they had enough integrity to say a decent word about plays with a sincere, human story illustrating that kindness is better than a warped nature, showing that the latter causes only suffering and misery. To show crime and violence as something not to be abhorred is a complete betrayal of all human decency.

We are often asked to do a thriller. I am not averse to thrillers. I do not agree that really unsavoury subjects should be dealt with in children's theatre. I am not narrow but I do think adults have a moral responsibility to the young. A point which makes thrillers less attractive to us is the fact that most thrillers have very small casts.

In 1956 we did Agatha Christie's *Ten Little Niggers*. The day after we decided to, the *Manchester Evening News* rang me to say they had had a call from a member of the public who said he was a patron of the Theatre, and was disgusted at our decision to do this thriller. I was asked to comment. I agreed to do so provided the paper would publish. I told them to tell their readers that whatever we decided to do, whenever we decided to do it and wherever we decided to do it, someone was disgusted. So, to keep our sanity, we made our plans, and went straight ahead.

One of my most exciting productions was the modern Passion Play, *A Man Dies*. I saw the blurb about it in the *TV Times*, and as I am always interested in seeing anything of an unusual nature, I prepared to watch it, but feeling certain I should not like it. To my surprise and delight I was very impressed. The impact remained with me, and I felt an impelling urge to produce it.

I was then invited by the Chester Diocesan Youth Committee to do a show for them. They had heard of this controversial and evocative play and suggested I did it. We gave two performances at the Chester Training College and two in Altrincham. It made a strong impression, on our audiences, and I knew then we would just *have* to do it at the Theatre.

As a general rule Theatre in the Round does not please me. But it can be effective. Here above all was a play that demanded this method of production. It was the only form that would bring out the full power of the structure.

To produce this play you need a fair-sized arena, and steps from it to a platform. We arranged the audience on three sides of the arena, the fourth side being the stage. No scenery was used. The bareness added to the atmosphere. A centre gangway led from the back of the theatre to the arena. On the cyclorama was directed a blue flood—bordering on purple—and from stage left a beam of light from an ordinary slide projector was directed across the stage, hitting the cyclorama up right in an oval shape. In the projector was a slide showing three crosses in silhouette. Spots were directed on the arena, on centre stage, on the Reader, and on each of the two singers. Each spot was connected to a separate dimmer.

The cast was in modern dress. Christ, played by a nineteen-year-old boy, wore jeans and a mohair pullover. The guards wore leather motor-cycling jackets and crash helmets. The rest were in their own clothes.

On the stage, up left, were two boys playing guitars and a third on the drums. Just inside the proscenium arch left was a girl singer, and on stage right was a boy singer. In front of the proscenium, on the left was a boy reader. Down in the arena the crowd was massed.

From the first rehearsal it was a most exciting venture. We had forty-five in the cast, varying from seven-year-olds to one of twenty-two.

There were moments of exceptional poignancy. Probably the greatest was when the crowd was split up into groups. Two small boys were blowing up a football. Two tiny girls were dressing a doll. Three older girls were fitting on a dress. Four fifteen-year-old boys were filling in football coupons. Another lad was drinking from a bottle, on a bench a boy and girl were spooning. One group was playing cards. Others were jiving.

Christ appeared at the top of the steps holding a chalice. A beam of light picked him out. As he stood there for a moment, Walford Davies's 'Solemn Melody' was faded in, played on an organ. Christ looked sadly on the motley crowd beneath him. Then, as the lights came up on the kaleidoscopic picture, Christ slowly came down the steps, and gliding among the groups, each busy with its own preoccupation, he offered the chalice to each group in turn. Not one paid the slightest notice, but continued with what they were doing, not even turning a head. Having approached every group, he solemnly turned, climbed the steps, and followed by the spotlight, passed out of sight. At the same time light and music gradually faded out. Then followed one of those pregnant silences that producers dream about.

One lady, who came to see all the four performances, assured me that, when this scene ended, she had to go out of the theatre to compose herself, she was so moved. Three of our smaller boys in the crowd were most impressed because four elderly ladies in the audience openly wept.

I was asked to take part in a one-day conference on Drama in Education at Sedgeley Park Training College about ten days before we presented *A Man Dies*. It was suggested that I take along with me a group from our Theatre and let the delegates see some of our work. I explained that all I could offer would be an uninterrupted rehearsal of *A Man Dies*.

As Sedgeley Park College is a Catholic College, I was a little hesitant, feeling that this modern idiom might not go down too well. I put forward this view but was assured that they would welcome the performance. So we duly gave the performance. It was a thrilling experience for my youngsters. The audience, mostly teachers, many of them nuns and priests, sat engrossed by the play's message. After, many who had watched came to express their appreciation.

When we presented it in our Theatre I noticed in the audience a group of girls from a well-known Catholic school in Manchester. On talking to the teachers in charge, I found that the principal of their school had seen the performance at Sedgeley Park. She had told her staff that when she found we were going to do it at the Training College Conference, she had turned up prepared to hate it. So impressed had she been, that she wanted her senior girls to see it. As I look back on this play, I feel it was one of the most satisfying productions I have ever done.

We did Ian Hay's *The Housemaster*. This proved a most enjoyable effort since it has such a gay atmosphere. It deals with the upset caused in a boys' boarding school, when three young girls arrive unexpectedly to live with the housemaster. The situation is such that any young person either in the cast or in the audience will revel in the hilarious events on the stage. To present this with a young cast gives the make-up department an excellent opportunity to display its talent.

We had the pleasure of doing an original play by a local playwright. It was *The Green Planet* by Frank Harris, an amusing piece about space travel.

A rocket is released before it is due to start, and much amusement ensues. The crew land on the Green Planet where illness is unknown, and find themselves in some awkward and dangerous situations. The main humour is supplied by a slick American film producer, Washington P. Schnitzel, and his camera-man,

Mr Harris has very kindly agreed to donate fifty per cent of all royalties to our Theatre. Anyone interested in this show should contact me personally.

There is often an outcry that there is a dearth of plays suitable for youth theatre. It is usually made by people who have a preconceived notion of what young people ought to like. This, to my mind, is the wrong way to look at the problem. Introduce all kinds of plays to your young people, and you will be amazed at the response. Furthermore, at the present time many good writers are working in this field, and I am confident that in the very near future we shall have some excellent plays to tackle.

Alice, Thomas and Jane was an amusing, exciting little play.

The story concerns the three children of a scientist. The Spanish onion boy steals some important papers belonging to the scientist. The children find out and decide to get the papers back. The chase leads them to France. Excitement and humour mount up to a fine denouement.

The lead was a tiny Irish girl of nine. She had a most bewitching smile and a vivacious personality. Within two minutes of appearing on the stage she had the audience in the palm of her hand. She never let them go until curtain fall. At the end our little Alice received a richly deserved ovation for a delightful performance.

Those sour, clever pontificating know-alls who declare that such an experience as Alice had does harm should have seen the humble way in which she accepted the applause. She remained the same sweet, shy, pleasant little girl she always had been. At the moment she is doing well in the sixth form of a very good school, and is likely to be a teacher. She will be all the richer for her happy experience in *Alice, Thomas and Jane*.

I I

Administration

From our very first meeting on that April night in 1945 we determined that the Theatre should be conducted on businesslike lines.

During the first two years, quite understandably, meetings were frequent, and often at very short notice, just as the exigencies of the moment demanded. Snags of varied intensity soon reared their heads, like the snakes of Medusa's hair. Many of them had to be dealt with on the instant. In those days the phone sizzled. Looking back, I am sure we enjoyed the hurly-burly, cut-and-thrust atmosphere of this teething period. We were tempered in the fire, and many later difficulties have been robbed of their terrors. Gradually, and with great care, we hacked out an efficient constitution which has successfully served us for several years.

We are registered under the Friendly Societies' Act 1896 to 1948. Our registered office is at the Headquarters, 28 Talbot Road, Old Trafford, Manchester, 16.

We have three grades of membership: Juniors, 7 years of age to 16 years; Intermediates, 16 to 18 years; Seniors, 18 to 25 years. These groups are specifically acting members. Anyone may join as a supporting member.

Since our foundation in 1945 to March 1966, Junior members have paid a shilling per annum membership fee, Intermediates one and sixpence and Seniors three shillings. Owing to increased expenses in every department of the Theatre, from 1st April, 1966, the subscriptions have been as follows: Juniors, two shillings; Intermediates, three shillings and sixpence; Seniors, five shillings. Our aim has always been to keep our subscriptions as low as possible so that no interested youngster is kept away because he or she cannot afford to join.

It is a rule that any member who has not paid his subscription by December 31st in any year, shall cease to be a member of the Theatre. If he has not paid his subscription by August 31st in any year, he shall be ineligible to hold office, or to take part in any production. Furthermore, he shall forfeit his power to vote at the Annual, or Extra-ordinary General, Meeting. The Annual General Meeting is held not later than March 31st, at the headquarters.

An Extra-ordinary General Meeting is held whenever there is sufficient cause. One may be called whenever twenty-eight members, of whom not more than twenty-five per cent are under eighteen years old, request so, in writing, to the Secretary. At all General Meetings the Chairman, or Vice-Chairman, presides, and five members make a quorum.

The affairs of the Theatre are controlled by an Executive Committee, which meets at least once every month. This group consists of the Chairman, Vice-Chairman, Secretary, Treasurer, Director of Productions, Business Manager and seven Committee members, three of whom must be Inter-mediate members. All officers must be over sixteen years of age. The same person cannot be Secretary or Treasurer, and also a Trustee of the Theatre.

There are three Trustees. The Chairman, Alderman Harry Lord, CBE, JP, CC, the Vice-Chairman, Miss Blodwyn Williams, and myself. The Trustees hold office during the pleasure of the Society. All other officers hold their posts for one year. At the Annual General Meeting they can be re-elected for a further term of office. Should any officer resign, or the office be vacated for any reason, the Executive Committee has power to fill the office until the next Annual General Meeting, when it is voted for in the usual way.

The Treasurer takes charge of any funds not invested. He pays the bills when sanctioned by the Executive Committee to whom he presents an account of the monetary affairs of

G

the Theatre. He produces all documents when requested, and arranges the annual audit with the Auditor chosen by the Executive Committee. The Secretary attends all meetings of the Executive Committee, making a record of all proceedings at each. These are read at the next meeting and signed by the Chairman after being passed as a correct record by the assembled members. The Secretary summons and gives notice of all meetings of the Theatre, and generally acts under the direction of the Executive Committee.

Any three members can call a special Executive Committee Meeting, by giving seven clear days' notice in writing to the Secretary. At that meeting only the business specified in the notice can be dealt with.

We have five sub-committees. They are: Front of House Committee; Social and Catering Committee; Productions Committee; Wardrobe Committee; Scenery and Props Committee. Each committee appoints its own chairman and secretary. Such appointments are notified to the Executive Committee. No sub-committee can enter into any financial commitments or determine policies without the consent of the Executive Committee.

The duties of the Front of House Committee are as follows: distribution and sale of advance, and door tickets; seating arrangements; provision of stewards; promotion of other events, such as raffles, during the run of a production.

The Social and Catering Committee organizes the catering at social functions at the headquarters. They attend to refreshments for the stage staff, the cast and any visitors, such as the press at dress rehearsal and on the evenings of the actual production. Further to these they deal with the refreshments sold to patrons during the intervals of the show.

The Director of Productions is responsible for the selection of productions. He recommends them to the Productions Committee, consisting of Stage Manager, Assistant Stage Manager, Wardrobe Mistress, Property Mistress, Designer and certain co-opted members. The recommendations are reviewed from the point of view of costumes required, scenery and props, royalties and subject matter of the plot. A rough estimate of the cost is prepared and the whole presented to the Executive Committee for consideration and approval.

The Wardrobe Committee is responsible for the making and maintenance of the costumes. The Wardrobe Mistress deals with the Costume Hire Service.

Scenery and Property Committee is of course responsible for the making and maintenance of scenery and properties. They build the scenery and arrange for transportation where necessary. The Stage Manager deals with the hiring out of scenery and properties.

There is also a House Committee which is responsible for events happening in the Headquarters. Any rehearsal, committee meeting or gathering of any kind must be arranged with the approval of this committee.

In 1965 our Intermediate and Senior members each formed a small committee, with a view to making money for the Theatre. They are now contemplating special efforts for the Building Fund.

The full Constitution, printed in small book form, is available at a shilling to members. one and sixpence to non-members. Anyone wanting one should post one and ten-pence to the Secretary at the Headquarters.

Should you start a Children's Theatre group of any form, I strongly recommend the drawing up of a sound constitution in the early days. It will take time and thought, but the smooth working of the group will be ample reward for the effort made.

STRETFORD CHILDREN'S THEATRE

To Hon. Secretary,
28, Talbot Road,
Old Trafford, Manchester, 16.

Date..........................

I desire to apply for

I desire to apply for a renewal of my membership of the Stretford Children's Theatre for.............and enclose herewith

my membership fee as under.

*1/6 for a Junior 7 to 16 years of age.

2/6 for an Intermediate 16 to 18 years of age.

*5/- for an Adult.

*Please cross out the lines which do not apply.

Can you assist in any of the Theatre's activities if we should require your help?

Can you assist the Wardrobe Committee to make costumes, hats etc? ....

Can you assist in making scenery and the properties of the stage? ....

Can you assist in painting the scenery? ....

Can you assist in making-up players? ....

Can you assist in 'Front of House' Management? ....

NAME (in block capitals) ....   If the applicant is under 18 please state date of birth ....

ADDRESS ....   What School do you attend? ....

(Application form for membership)

12

Finances

As I have said, we founded the Theatre with not a farthing
in the kitty. Seven people on an evening in 1945 had enough
faith in my ideas to start the scheme. We realized we would
have to be practical. We would have to conjure money from
somewhere. On that point we had no illusions.

We soon received some donations. The first was a guinea
from Mr Charles Hamilton, who in 1965 became a Stretford
Councillor. I have always been grateful for that guinea. Other
donations followed, not in a rush, but they were an encouragement. The first steady money to come our way was the
subscriptions of the members. These have always been small.

During the first few years we ran a series of whist drives,
beetle drives, dances, coffee mornings and social evenings.
Times change, and these types of efforts seem out of favour
today. Individual sympathizers do still hold functions in
their homes.

One form of making money never seems to lose its attraction. At every show, at every performance, we raffle something. Human nature being what it is, few people can resist
the lure of the raffle ticket, unless religious convictions pro-
hibit participation. It is amazing what objects are given us to
raffle. A set of false teeth was once sent to us. We felt few
would buy tickets for them so they were quietly cremated.

I must mention one of our great benefactors in the realm
of raffles. Some twelve years ago I received a donation via
the post from a Mr Ash. I did not know anyone of that
name. On investigating, I found he had a jeweller's shop quite
near the Civic Theatre. I called to thank him. He assured me

of his sincere desire to help the theatre. From that day, whenever we had a show he gave us something to raffle. After his tragic death that we all felt as a personal loss, his widow has generously undertaken to continue Mr Ash's custom. Such generosity is heart-warming.

Occasionally we conduct a larger competition. A very popular contest is a Stop-Watch Competition. This is a profitable method of raising money, if it is properly organized.

A series of 720 cards is printed. Each card represents one minute of twelve hours. For example, at the top of the card may be printed 'Ten hours, seven minutes'. Then there are sixty lines on each card, numbered from one to sixty. Each line represents a second. We charge a penny a line. On each line is written the name of the donor. Thus your line may read 'Seven hours, five minutes, ten seconds'.

A watch is wound up, set at twelve o'clock and sealed in a box. It is most satisfactory to have a fixed period for selling the cards. A month is about right. If one can enlist, say, fifty people to help, the cards are distributed and the campaign starts. When the cards are collected, the watch is taken out of the box and the reading checked. The person whose name is on the second when the watch stopped is the winner. We usually allow the winner to choose a watch to the value of twenty-five pounds. Should there be no name on the exact line, the name on the first line after the exact line is counted as the winner.

The cards cost about five pounds a set. If every line is sold one hundred and eighty pounds are collected. With costs around thirty pounds, a profit of a hundred and fifty pounds is possible. To run a scheme of this kind, it is necessary to get a licence, costing a guinea. One such licence is allowed each year, and is obtainable from the Town Hall.

For years the City Fathers watched our efforts. When they saw we meant business, and were achieving results, they made a generous gesture. They gave us a grant of a hundred pounds. They have given this grant each year since, and to help us when we were faced with a huge repair bill for the roof they increased it to one hundred and seventy-five pounds. It is most gratifying to know that some of our Council representatives are interested in the arts. Many people who are struggling to keep alive the flame of artistic endeavours do not know that it is the law of the land that local Councils are empowered to levy up to a sixpenny rate for 'cultural development within the borough'. Some Councils do not want their ratepayers to know this. Thank God some Stretford people do realize the arts are necessary for the full development of the human spirit.

This help, for which we are most grateful, has enabled us to continue our work with benefit to our members, and pleasure to thousands of our patrons.

In nineteen sixty-six our coming of age year, we inaugurated our patron scheme. Every patron subscribing a guinea receives a booklet containing six vouchers. Each voucher can be exchanged for an adult ticket for any show during the season.

Some years ago, I inaugurated a scheme to collect one million half-pennies. We collected a few thousand, and then, because of my multifarious duties, I could not continue with it and it has ceased to function. Some energetic person could resurrect this plan. How I long for a dozen keen adult helpers to deal with the many things which are screaming to be taken in hand!

At different crises in our history we have had some exceptional benefactors, notably our Chairman Alderman Harry Lord and the late Mrs Lord when we bought the Headquarters. Alderman Lord has on more than one occasion helped us financially. In 1964 when we were faced with an enormous repair bill, he guaranteed us an overdraft of five hundred pounds.

Since the acquisition of our headquarters, our expenses have increased. Gas, electricity, water rate, ground rent, and, during the last few years, rates, all make our annual expenditure high. Add to these repairs and the cost of our productions. Each show we do costs over a hundred pounds.

We sold a small part of our garden behind the Headquarters. This was wanted for development by a business firm. With the money we made certain improvements in the Headquarters, and had over a little sum to put in the bank. This, and more, was swallowed up when we had to have a new roof.

In 1965 we had a pleasant surprise. Mr Jenkinson, who was the owner of Trojan Electric, arranged a settlement, part of which was donated to charities. We received a cheque for fifty pounds. Would that other industrialists looked upon us with such comprehending generosity!

Another benefactor who has untiringly given of his time to further the interests of the Theatre is Mr Percy Lord, Chief Education Officer for the County of Lancaster. He came to open our 1961 season. When he addressed the audience, he expressed surprise that we had never asked the county for financial aid. This was soon remedied and to our great delight we received a handsome cheque from the County Education Committee. In 1964 when we were compelled to have a new roof, we were sorely harassed. Our Chairman came forward as I have already explained. He agreed that there were other things which needed attending to.

Our heating was faulty and gave a great deal of trouble with poor results. We had gas fires installed. Our garden was always untidy so this was asphalted.

We drew out all we had in the bank, and found we were nearly five hundred pounds in the red. This was alarming, but in our usual optimistic spirit we set about trying to make some money.

We received the cheque from the Council. Then Mr Percy Lord began to harass the Ministry on our behalf. After several months and many letters, the answers remained firm negatives. To keep up our morale the County Education Committee sent us the cheque I have mentioned. At long last, after many people had added their exhortations, including the then Member of Parliament for Stretford, Sir

Samuel Storey, and continued effort on the part of Mr
Percy Lord, we received a cheque for over three hundred
pounds from the Ministry. Together with Mr Jenkinson's
gift and patrons' guineas, we were out of the red in the
second half of 1965. We shall always remember Mr Percy
Lord with sincere gratitude.

We are now in the happy position of having a few pounds
in the bank. I am getting older, and I can foresee the time
when I shall have to relinquish the work in the Theatre. I
trust I shall have many more years, but in the fullness of
time I shall have to face this eventuality. I have one wish of
great importance left. That is to see a Building Fund in
existence. We have always had in mind a theatre of our very
own. Had we had the support of all the schools in Stretford
we need never have lost a farthing on any of our productions.
As it is we must have lost hundreds. I find this a terrible
thing to contemplate. We are still trying to make a few
pounds from jumble sales, sales of work, raffles, and such
efforts.

It makes me angry to think of the way money is literally
thrown about in the gambling clubs, shooting up like
mushrooms, and yet the arts cannot develop their full
potentialities because of the lack of a few thousands. What
does one do to catch the eye of a benevolent millionaire? I
wish I knew.

I cannot leave this chapter without a special reference to
two individuals who have helped us in our financial difficulties.

Mr Reg Codd, chief clerk in the Town Clerk's Department
in the Stretford Town Hall, is. like myself, a native of Lincolnshire. He, with his friend, Mr Arthur Dunn, has for
many years run a series of dances at Longford Hall for
charities. When Mr Codd found out I was also a 'Yellowbelly', he became interested in the Children's Theatre
and for several years now they have included the Theatre
in their programme of charities, with the result that they
have donated hundreds of pounds to further our work. They

will never really know what this has meant to us. Our thanks can only show a mite of our gratitude.

For many years the Baths Superintendant, Mr Harry Lightfoot, was our Treasurer. He worked ceaselessly and selflessly for our interests, and his efforts only came to an end at his decease. This coincided with his retirement.

His colleagues in the Town Hall had subscribed for a testimonial. On his sudden death, Mrs Lightfoot said she would like this sum to be used in connection with one of the many organizations to which he had given so much of his time and interest. She agreed that a shield should be purchased in his memory and given to the Theatre. So, each year, the Harry Lightfoot Shield is presented to the boy who has given the outstanding performance of the year. He holds the shield for one year.

Over the years we have been very fortunate in having some excellent honorary auditors. The present one is Mr S. R. Johnson, FIMTA, FSAA, Borough Treasurer, to whom we are most grateful.

13

Headquarters

When I was building my castles, I had visualized sumptuous headquarters. They would be the last word in design and equipment. I thought of those dreams on the night we founded the Theatre. We had no meeting place. As with the parents of the Immortal Child, there was no room.

There is no worse feeling than that one has no home. Committee members were kind. They allowed us to hold meetings in their homes. But I felt we were wanderers. When I moaned about our lack, I was told to be patient. I felt that we must have a place of our own before we could really achieve anything worth-while.

Our Wardrobe Mistress was using a bedroom as the Wardrobe. It was quickly filling up and the door would only just open. Nor were the costumes sufficiently accessible. Props were everywhere. My garden shed was crammed with the most amazing collection of weird articles. Scenery was made in one place and stored in another.

By varied means, by untold thought and effort, often doing things at which we really jibbed, we had accumulated nearly five hundred pounds. This was not enough to buy, but we were ready to rent, premises. We advertised and received a list of addresses of rooms to let.

A section of the Committee visited all these. Never have I seen such depressing places. Grim, dismal, foul-smelling, they repelled me, and sent my spirits plummeting. Out in all weathers, we tramped round parts of Stretford I did not know existed. Had some of us been shanghaied or murdered, it would have been no surprise. And the result was a complete blank.

Then in 1954 we heard of a house which from all accounts would be ideal. It was perfectly sited, and although it required many adjustments, would provide us with a headquarters where we could do what we had set out to do.

The house was occupied by the Ministry of Food. Powdered milk, orange juice and similar concoctions were distributed to waiting parents. Rumour stated that it was to be derequisitioned in the very near future. For once, rumour was correct. We found out the name of the owner, contacted him, and an interview was arranged for a Sunday morning, at the house.

The owner proved to be a genial person, who explained that this house had been his home. It was the last part of the family property, and because of the requisitioning by the Government, they had been unable to sell it. Once it was free they wished to get rid of it, and so wind up the family's affairs.

We wandered through the rooms, most of them fitted up as offices. Partitions and counters loomed everywhere. There were good cellars, and plenty of rooms for our various departments. At the rear of the house was a concrete hut which I saw had great possibilities. The siting of the building was most convenient. Across the road was the Old Trafford Station. Round the corner was a bus stop serving all services into and out of the city one way, and Stretford the other.

I came away from that first interview with my head reeling. We *must* have this house. A home of our own would double the efficiency of our work. Again the question—what about money? A further meeting had been arranged on a date giving us time to talk the whole thing over.

Schemes sane and preposterous chased themselves around my brain. All I knew was that we must find ways and means of getting that house. All our work would be truncated and much of it would be stillborn until we had a home.

The next meeting was again on a Sunday morning. The

actual date when the house was to be vacated was now known. It was three months hence. We had not much time.

I remember the owner standing with me on that second Sunday in the front garden. In my mind's eye we already owned it. The owner told me he had a son who was a schoolmaster. The latter had heard our story and had urged his father to let us have the house. As the relinquishing date was so near, the Ministry of Food official was present. When we were discussing various details, the Ministry official pointed out that during their tenancy dry rot had been discovered. Steel girders and brick columns had displaced rotten wood. Then he dropped a bombshell. The Ministry had built the hut at the back and said if we wanted that then we would have to purchase that separately. The owner had quoted two thousand pounds for the house, and we had supposed the hut was included.

Our chairman is a very astute man. He looked at me, winked, and told the owner that if that was the case, the deal was off, as the hut would be of exceptional use to us. A thought then flashed across my mind. It is amazing how quickly one can become a bargaining animal when a quick decision is demanded. The announcement by our chairman had stopped the spate of conversation. It felt as though creation was holding its breath. Like a hot glow, the idea which had come to me, filled my mind. Then, *mirabile dictu*, the man from the Ministry made the suggestion which I was bursting to voice.

He reminded us that, according to regulations, they would have to leave the house as they had found it. Amongst other things they would have to paint it outside. If we were not prepared to buy the hut then it would have to be pulled down. That would cost a bit, and they would get nothing for the sections. They might even have to pay to have them removed. It seemed pointless to pull it down at this expense when we could use it. He then suggested that we might like to accept it in lieu of the decoration. Just the idea I had wanted to propose. Of course, this was most acceptable,

Then, in an agony of mind, because I felt we must not let this opportunity slip by, and having no idea where the money was coming from, I asked the owner if he would drop his price, as we would now have to stand the cost of having the house painted. After a short, friendly discussion we came to terms at the figure of seventeen hundred pounds.

I went home on air, but it was tinged with frost. Where on earth were we to get seventeen hundred pounds and at the same time continue our activities? Had we been rash? Why had I ever started this avalanche?

Now started a series of frantic meetings. Certain Committee members were far from happy. Who could blame them? With the painting of the house which would have to be done to preserve the house, we were committed to the tune of about two thousand pounds.

One member tremblingly pointed out that, having got the house, there would be the running costs. Electricity, gas, water, rates. Yes, on contemplation it was frightening. Boldly I pointed out that many people had expressed doubts when we founded the Theatre. Here we were nine years later still going strong. I felt my voice did not sound too confident.

Schemes to get the money were now suggested. It was proposed we floated a loan. Little enthusiasm was evinced. I favoured a mortgage. I argued that we could raise the deposit. Then we could enlist the help of people who would give a small weekly sum to meet the monthly sum required. I still think that would have been a feasible scheme. We went on arguing, sifting and rejecting for some weeks. Then, when going to yet another meeting, I was met at the door by the Chairman, who genially told me to stop worrying, as he had found a solution. When he expounded the scheme, I gasped with disbelief. I could not realize that such good fortune had come our way.

Our chairman and his wife were willing to lend us thirteen hundred pounds, free of interest, for as long as we liked. We took most of our little nest egg out of the bank and added four hundred to the loan. We still had sufficient to start off the next season.

Negotiations with solicitors and other impressive-looking people were put in motion, and in a few weeks, there we were, with a home of our own. I just could not feel it was a reality.

We explained the situation to our young members. I stressed the point that we must pay back this loan at the very earliest moment. Setting to with a will, by blood, sweat, and tears, we paid back our benefactors in under six years.

A local contractor gave us a flagpole, and on Saturday, 24th September, 1960, I had the honour of hoisting the Union Jack to denote our freedom from debt. In the evening we had a special function. All who had helped the Theatre in any way were invited. The Mayor, Councillor H. Armitage, JP, accepted the deeds on behalf of the Theatre. It was one of the proudest moments in our history.

Mr Arnold Hancock, Solicitor, of Spring Gardens, Manchester, prepared all the necessary documents, and presented them to the Theatre as a gift. He has remained our honorary solicitor, and this generous service we have deeply appreciated. This is another example of public spirit, extended to us by someone who believes in us.

June Ritchie happened to be home on holiday, and gave us examples of her talent. In all respects it was a memorable evening.

We set to work to spend some effort on the building to make it more beautiful and useful. We never cease in these tasks. It is difficult to do what I would like because we are hort-staffed. but we continually try.

14

Advertising

If you are engaged in presenting shows on either the professional or the amateur stage, your very first aim, after making sure your production is of the highest quality, is to see you do not lose money if you can possibly help it. One has to be practical on this point.

The way to ensure solvency is to sell tickets. Empty seats, or a 'paper' house, (an audience made up of holders of complimentary tickets) will not pay your rent, the royalties on the play or buy materials to make scenery and costumes. Another point worth considering is that empty seats are bad for the morale of your company.

You will not fill your seats if no one knows about your show. It is your primary concern to see that as many people as possible know when and where your forthcoming production is to be staged.

Advertising is expensive, but it must be done. If you are enterprising, it is possible to get quite a lot gratis. Your local paper is there to let the residents in your area know what is happening around them. Once let your local reporters know that you are doing something worth noting, then you need never fear that your activities will be missed. I have had four calls from papers and news agencies today, to ask me if I have anything interesting to tell them about our production next week. Any interesting anecdote about your organization would be of interest to the newsmen.

Last October we produced *Twelfth Night*. In this play the two characters Sebastian and Viola are twins. Frequently when this play is presented, these two characters look anything but twins. In our production they were taken by a brother and siter. Whilst not twins, they were sufficiently alike to look more convincing twins than is usual in productions of *Twelfth Night*. This fact was enough interest to the local paper for them to put a paragraph in the paper about it. This was publicity. Publicity is the life-blood of a theatre. Once neglect to let the public know what you are doing and you are doomed to extinction, unless you can find a wealthy patron.

When we plan a new season, we let the papers know our programme. If we make a change in policy or decide on any new venture, then the pressmen are informed.

Sometimes a special feature is made in a particular production about one of our departments. It may be that we are doing some special costumes, or some awkward property is giving us trouble. When we did *Rumpelstiltskin* we needed a spinning-wheel. The press put this out for us, and it was actually the wife of one of the drama critics on an evening paper who lent us the very type of wheel we wanted.

In the *Willow Pattern Dream* we wanted a real pekinese dog. Again the press advertised for us. We got the dog. Furthermore, the lady who owned it bred pekes. She was so delighted that her dog had helped us she gave it to me. I would dearly have liked to accept, but I had a dog at home. It was a very jealous animal and, had I taken the little peke home, murder would have been committed. I explained to the lady, and she allowed me to give it to one of our girls.

We usually depute two members to be responsible for the publicity. We have not organized it as well as we should like, but this has not been possible because of shortage of help. Because of this deficiency individuals have had too much to do.

For every show we have about two hundred posters and a thousand handbills printed. All these are distributed throughout the borough. Every school receives a notice and a booking form. During the last four seasons we have had large posters on three railway sites. These are fairly expensive costing us eight pounds.

H

It is possible for posters to be done in the art lesson if one could find a head teacher who would co-operate. We have also hired a loudspeaker van and toured the district.

Of course if you can get on the radio or on television, you have a vast audience. I did my first broadcast about the Theatre in November, 1945, when we had just started. On 22nd May, 1957, in the programme *Youth Wants to Know* at the Granada Studios in Manchester we took part in the edition of this series entitled, 'Don't put your daughter on the stage, Mrs Worthington'. About fifty of our members took part.

In July, 1963, on the Home Service programme, in the series People Today, I and some of the youngsters broadcast. This was repeated in January, 1965, and gave us great publicity. It was produced, brilliantly, I considered, by Geoffrey Howard. We again appeared on television in ABC at Large when we did *The Lady's not for Burning*.

We are often mentioned in magazines like *Lancashire Life*, and local clubs and churches display our posters on their notice boards.

Our social activities result in newspaper reports. The Lancashire Education Department issue a glossy magazine entitled *Lancashire Education*. I am asked to contribute news of our activities. The well-known magazine *Amateur Stage* welcomes particulars of shows for inclusion in their notices of forthcoming productions in the amateur world. We always send particulars of shows to the BBC in Manchester for inclusion in The Week Ahead. We have attempted to issue a news sheet called *Tabs Away*. It went for a few issues and I am hoping to revive it soon. I would like a new issue at each production.

It is necessary in this age of screaming headlines and public probes into the idiosyncrasies of private lives to keep your notices constantly hammered out in any way you can. The butterfly minds of the public seldom settle for above two or three seconds on any topic.

Our new idea of going on tour will prove of much value.

It will complement the lecturing I do about our work. As we generally keep a pictorial record of each show, I am able to illustrate my lectures. I visit Training Colleges, Townswomen's Guilds, Women's Institutes, Rotary Clubs, churches and similar organizations.

15

Rehearsals

Once the important task of casting is complete, then rehearsals begin. The success or failure of these depends entirely on the producer. It is he who is in control. In the case of a youth theatre, the producer is even more important than in an adult group. His influence is all the greater in many ways. If he knows his job, is firm but kindly, and above all confident, then a successful production will be possible. If his grasp is feeble, indecisive, or erratic, then an unsatisfying, muddled, weak picture will emerge.

Apart from the barest fundamentals, a good producer will develop a personal rehearsal method. It will have on it his own stamp. It would be unworkable in the hands of anyone else. This is a perfectly natural development. His ideas and methods will grow from his personality.

I have been fortunate in many ways. I have, apart from one or two one-act plays, produced all the shows since the Theatre was founded. I have largely directed the policy, and have been able to build up what is, in effect, a repertory company.

Whilst my acting personnel is constantly changing, thus preventing staleness, I do retain a nucleus of members who work with me from, say, three to ten years. This enables the core of my company to become thoroughly acquainted with me and my methods. They also get to know each other and how to develop their individual abilities. At the same time I get to know their capabilities, and what is very important, their idiosyncrasies. I have ample opportunity to develop their potentialities, to encourage the timid and on occasion to check the over-exuberant.

Having headquarters of our own has meant a more pleasant, relaxed and uninterrupted atmosphere. This is most valuable to both myself and cast. We have, over the years, constructed an atmosphere of happy, concentrated effort. I hasten to point out that the operative word is 'effort'. We enjoy our work, and it is *work*.

Anyone who joins our Theatre with the idea of fooling about and upsetting others is in for a shock, Whoever it is, is quickly sized up, and I myself have little to do with the ultimate fate of that member. The cast, by varied and often unusual methods, make it clear that such an attitude is alien to our tradition.

I am anxious that our members should be happy and enjoy themselves, but no slack, casual attitude is tolerated for a second. Such an approach to stage work is disastrous.

By the end of a season I have formulated a programme for the next. This plan is discussed at length with the Production Committee. We deal with the first play in detail and decide on the sets. We deal with the other productions more leisurely. Once the Production Committee has come to a decision, it is placed before the Executive Committe for approval. When this is given, casting takes place.

Before rehearsals start, I soak myself in the play. Often I have several notebooks filled with jottings of every description. There are sketches of costumes, scenery, furniture props, moves and ideas to be tried out.

I read through the script many times. The first three or four times will give me a good picture of the plot, and a fair idea of at least the main characters. Then I read it through with a particular aspect in mind. It may be the lighting, the costumes, the reactions between two or three of the characters. Gradually from my reading and notes emerges my main production plan.

This basic plan must be in the producer's mind before the first rehearsal. It must not be so crystallized as to be fossilized.

It should be flexible and capable of adjustment when rehearsals bring unexpected snags or flashes of inspiration. Such events are common, making rehearsals exciting experiences, stimulating and vital: renewed thrills every time we meet.

Apart from musicals and Shakespearean productions, I take seven to eight weeks to rehearse a full-length play. With the exceptions it may extend to ten weeks. Many people express surprise at the shortness of the period. A dreary, extended period of rehearsal only results in a dreary, lifeless production.

To plead that a cast will not turn up to two or three rehearsals a week is usually the sign of a weak producer. It could be complete lack of interest on the part of the cast. If this is so, cancel the show. I find little trouble in this direction. My members are so keen, that many of them would live at the headquarters if I would allow it. In our rehearsal period, we have twenty to twenty-four rehearsals. Again let me say, when we meet, we *work*.

When a member is cast for a part and accepts, then he must agree to our rehearsal procedure. I have a private chat with each member of the cast and particularly with new members, pointing out their obligations.

I hold myself at the disposal of the cast as to when we hold rehearsals. We have a meeting to fix the evenings most convenient to the majority, and a full rehearsal time-table. Mondays and Thursdays seem to be the most popular. It may be, that because of unusual circumstances, we can only settle a two or three weeks' schedule. If this is the case, we have another meeting later.

A copy of the rehearsal time-table is put on the notice-board and a copy given to each member of the cast. On this is clearly stated every date on which there is a rehearsal and exactly what we are going to do on that evening. Seldom do I change these particulars.

Members of the cast are expected to be punctual. We assemble at 7 o'clock and start rehearsing at 7.15. We continue until about 9.15. If the cast is made up of Senior members, then we go on until 10 o'clock. Then, whatever we are busy with, we stop. It is a rule that the Headquarters closes at ten unless it is being used for a function of a special nature.

Should any member of the cast miss a rehearsal, then he must let me know the reason within twenty-four hours. Failure to do this may easily result in the loss of his part. We work on such a tight schedule that I cannot be left in any doubt as to the exact state of affairs.

If a member of the cast finds out beforehand that he cannot attend any rehearsal, and he has a valid reason, then he comes to me and explains. I then alter the rehearsal schedule a little so as to minimize the effect on the rehearsal.

The cast must be prepared to attend two rehearsals a week as a minimum. Lately we have had such keen people, and they have worked so hard, that we have been doing our shows with a maximum of twenty rehearsals. I expect the cast to attend three rehearsals a week when necessary.

Having settled our rehearsal time-table, we then, at the first rehearsal, read through the entire play.

This means that the cast will now have an idea of the plot and characters, and any questions may be asked. We may have an extra evening to discuss the characterization and any matters which require a fuller explanation.

It is an understood thing that, during the first fortnight, it may be necessary to do a little recasting. It can happen that the potentialities of some of the cast may not materialize. It is then necessary to recast. This possibility is explained fully before rehearsals begin.

Any member jo the Theatre may come along to watch the rehearsals, but they must observe one or two conditions. They must not sit chewing gum, nor must they talk. If they do, they are asked to leave the room.

I try to, explain in these early rehearsals, one or two very important points. I point out, for instance, that an actor who only possesses technique is a mere bag of tricks.

He must understand the part sufficiently to develop artistry and a real feeling for the character.

Before rehearsals start, I have begun to prepare my Prompt Book. This is just about the most important job the producer must do at the start of a production. Many amateur producers will not take the trouble to do this. It does take a great deal of time, and trouble, but it must be done if you want your production to have that stamp of efficiency for which every worth-while producer works. A well-prepared Prompt Book also gives authority to the producer.

I personally like a large Prompt Book. A thick exercise book is ideal. I take the script copy to pieces, and with adhesive tape, I stick each page of the script on alternate blank pages of the exercise book. On the blank page opposite the page of script I note every move of each character, sound effects, lighting, interval music and anything of importance to the running of the play.

To start with I pencil in my main moves. It is better to use pencil for this, because you will almost certainly find it necessary to alter your first ideas as rehearsals proceed, due to many reasons. Pencil can be easily erased, even more easily if you use a soft 2B or 3B pencil for this. I usually put in moves in lead pencil, lighting details in green, effects in red and music particulars in blue. If a producer is unsure of his moves and groupings, this subconsciously influences adversely the morale of the cast.

Names, addresses and phone numbers of anyone with anything to do with the production are entered in the Prompt Book. A space is left for general notes. This book is the blueprint of the whole production. Should the producer have to miss a rehearsal, then his deputy should take his place knowing that in the Prompt Book are all the details he requires to continue the rehearsal in the same way as the producer would have done.

The firm development of our methods over twenty-one years has paid rich dividends. We have built up a tradition and rehearsals follow a pattern with little diversion. It is both amusing and illuminating to hear members of two or three seasons' experience in the Theatre instructing 'freshers' in the niceties of our rules and regulations. Some of them may seem strict. They are not quite so circumscribing as they sound. Our members recognize the reasons behind our rules and cheerfully submit to them. Should there be any thought of changing a rule, or even a suggestion of a new one, a meeting is called, and the matter discussed. Everyone, down to the youngest member, is allowed to voice his opinion, and is given a full and fair hearing. Having listened to all the arguments, then the matter is voted on.

Given good reasons, youth, in the main, I find more amenable to discipline than many adults. I do a certain amount of production with adult groups, and they give me more headaches with more disappointing results than my youngsters.

Sometimes, of course, we have members who join for other reasons than a love of drama. Hard work quickly weeds them out, and they fall by the wayside.

I can honestly say, that since the Theatre was founded I have never seriously been let down. On one or two occasions awkward situations have had to be manœuvred, when lack of experience together with the pressures of modern life have caused perhaps a clash of loyalties. We have always managed to resolve these difficulties in a rational and happy manner. No organization, at any time, can expect to escape these difficulties, and here again is yet another challenge.

We cannot be surprised at our youngsters having confused ideas of loyalty when many adults act as they do. All of us who are in positions of trust in the world of youth must never forget that we are a daily example in front of our charges. They are watching us all the time, even though they may try to give the impression that they take no notice of us. This is not so.

As a teacher of forty years' experience I am frequently horrified by the attitude of students from the universities. I was recently told by a student on the threshold of a teaching career that he did not agree with the idea of loyalty in any way. He felt that loyalty was a sign of weakness. Such views, coming from a person in that position, are frightening to all idealists. Is it necessary to add that this particular student was a Maths-Science student?

To return to our rehearsals. Having got the first reading over, imperative questions asked and answered and a clear idea of the plot gained, we are ready to start work.

I constantly remind the cast that I cannot do any real rehearsing until they really get rid of their scripts. We can do much drafting, familiarizing ourselves with exits, entrances and main moves, but no details can be absorbed while a character has his mind on the problem of remembering his lines.

I have little real trouble in this respect. Books are dropped for Act One at the sixth rehearsal. Then as we progress with the rehearsals, more scenes are added and by about the tenth to twelfth rehearsal we are free of books.

The members know I expect this procedure. If they have not learned their lines, then they are prompted. This they do not like, so they get down to the task of learning the lines. There are no short cuts. Each person finds some personal solution to the problem. One of the best ways, I think, is to tape the dialogue on a tape recorder, omitting the part you are taking. Set the tape going, and speak your lines in the correct place. After a little practice you will find your speed of learning has increased.

It is clearly understood that should any member of the cast not reach the required standard in rehearsal, then a replacement is made. I am in a strong position in this sort of situation. With our large membership, there is always someone to step in at very short notice. This all helps towards conditioning the attitude of the cast.

At all times the reasons underlying our rules are explained fully to the members.

Our second rehearsal usually takes the form of reading through the first act 'on the floor'. This is arranged as near as possible to the size of the stage in the Civic Theatre. Furniture is placed in the same positions as it will be in the actual production and entrances are clearly marked.

From the first rehearsal, movements, inflexion of voice, attitudes of mind, indeed anything which can help at all to build up the character is carefully considered. I make it my chief consideration to make sure my actors do not just recite their lines. I want them to help me to develop their part. I do not want them to be simply an echo of me. If they were they would be cardboard automata. They must develop the character around their own personalities. I explain the character and situations as I see them. We discuss these, and between us we arrive at a real, live, acceptable person. I do my very best to develop the characters so that they can believe in them.

Too often I have seen a drama school crush a budding artist's personality and superimpose an artificial way of speech or movement, in order to fit in with some preconceived idea of a particular tutor. The result has been a cold, cardboard figure, which is unsatisfactory both to the actor concerned and to the audience watching his performance. It is just another example of so much in modern life—soulless and savage. Do not think I have a 'down' on drama schools, far from it. I only object to some.

One undeviating rule we follow is that whatever act we have scheduled on our rehearsal time-table, we do just that. However patchy it may be, we complete the act. Weaknesses may be so bad that I call an extra rehearsal for the people concerned before we are scheduled to do that act again. This rehearsal may be at my own house. Such attention repays the trouble taken.

By the time we reach the dress rehearsal, there is a feeling of confidence, and, what is very important, a pleasing flow which can never be achieved in any other way. Frequently when I am adjudicating, I have to watch performances which are patchy. This is often caused by spending too long in rehearsing one scene at the expense of others.

Our great aim at each rehearsal is to make sure we are nearer our goal when we finish than we were when we started. What thrills me most of all is the really hard work my boys and girls put into their rehearsing. All the time they struggle to improve and present a result with polish and beauty. We never quite reach our goal. Sometimes we are nearer to it than at others. I can say, in all sincerity, there is always a satisfying feeling of integrity in our work. It shows through the greasepaint and floodlights, and of this I am very proud.

Another of our rules which is found irksome to new members is the one forbidding chewing gum on the premises. I have always considered it a disgusting habit, and addicts are not always too particular where they park the gum after having exercised their jaws on it. Insistence on good manners at all times, and especially during rehearsals, is the order of the day.

The press favour us with their presence at rehearsals sometimes. Reporters and photographers watch us at work. I welcome the visits of either interested individuals or groups at rehearsal. I ask that they make a proper arrangement beforehand so as to prevent overcrowding.

We never put on a special act for anyone. We continue with what is scheduled for that night. Time is allowed for the visitors to ask both myself and the cast any questions they may feel like posing. Our girls make tea, and at tea break the visitors are served with tea and biscuits. Visitors on such occasions have been known to leave donations. These are always most acceptable.

Consistency is very important when dealing with young people. If I call a rehearsal to finish at 9.30, we finish dead on time, as I am very averse to erratic rehearsals. Members of the cast should not be kept until they are exhausted. Usually we get through the work planned, and have a little time left when we can deal with a difficult point, or experiment with 'business'.

Our basic rehearsal time-table follows the same lines as

those explained in the chapter on Shakespeare. In the case of a Musical or a Shakespeare the rehearsal pattern is slightly different. We spend more time in preparatory study before the actual rehearsals begin.

In the later rehearsals I interrupt as little as possible. At the end of a scene I discuss the notes I have made during the action. I prefer to speak quietly to individuals about their faults and only pass open comment on mistakes of a general nature. We do our utmost to pay careful attention to significant detail.

Repetition of a specific piece of dialogue and action can only be repeated so often, depending on the particular individuals concerned; there is a point when tension cracks. A producer should learn to spot this point, stop rehearsing that bit and move on. It can be continued on another occasion.

Sound effects, interval music, and props are discussed at length with the appropriate people. I leave these individuals to deal with their duties, but casually, now and then, inquire how they are progressing.

The prompter is a very important person. Too many societies leave this key-post vacant until the dress rehearsal, and then wonder why things go wrong. On our time-table, the prompt is on duty from the sixth rehearsal, if not before. This officer of the society should know the play even better than the producer. We usually have two prompts. This is a safeguard, and also humane. To prompt a three-act play is a most arduous undertaking. To ease the strain two prompts take an act in turn. This helps to make the job less arduous and is also a safe insurance if one should be ill. In rehearsal they prompt on alternate rehearsals, and so get to know the whole script.

In the early stages of rehearsal, the Property Mistress—for some unknown reason we seem to have a girl every show we do—starts to gather the props together. As soon as 'business' begins on the set, then props should be in evidence. Where they cannot be procured before the dress rehearsal, then substitutes must be arranged. As many props as can possibly be gathered together should be in use in rehearsals for at least a month before the dress rehearsal.

The zeal of my youngsters was clearly illustrated one very foggy evening last winter. The fog was one of Manchester's worst. I was staying in school for my tea and rang up my wife to have a chat. She said, 'Surely you don't expect any of them to turn up tonight?'

Several of the cast lived at some distance from our head-quarters. I felt I had to turn up, so that if anyone came they would find me there. To my surprise and delight eighty-five per cent of the cast appeared. We had a sound rehearsal and I got home about 11 o'clock. Every member of the cast who had not been able to get through had phoned my home to say they would be at the next rehearsal. Such loyalty is very precious to me.

A producer must keep his critical faculties alert every moment. He must allow nothing muddled to pass. Whilst welcoming suggestions from the cast, he should never permit an argument to develop.

When rehearsing, take great care with pauses. They are often more pregnant than words. They can convey more and make a stronger impact. If the player tends to be erratic, suggest counting seconds mentally so as to ensure a constant performance when utilizing a pause. Do not move the lips when counting!

I always make a strong point of having accurate cues. This is very important. To be slipshod over your cues is discourteous to your fellow artist and can cause havoc.

Should nerves develop, the producer must use great tact. He must soothe, encourage and help.

I am often asked how we deal with love scenes. I have a stock way of tackling these. I quietly explain what I want my players to do, then I do not bother much about kisses or embraces in the early rehearsals. Quietly I talk to the two artists concerned, but do not take a long time about it. Then, during the last few rehearsals, I introduce the business, taking great care that the rest of the cast do not make fun of it after the first time.

We are often congratulated about the tender, unobtrusive way we do our love scenes. After all, if young folk do not understand the language of love, it is a sad look-out for the human race. I just make use of what is there. That is the most, and the best, any producer can do.

I will finish this chapter with two pieces of advice, which I feel are important for producers to remember. A producer should never play a part in the play he is producing. When you are acting, you can never see the stage as a picture, and so miss many important points.

Never shatter the confidence of your cast. The cast may laugh at mistakes but never the producer. That does not mean that a producer has to be glum. Use laughter on any occasion you can. It is the best of lubricants But never be tempted to laugh at a player who is struggling against nerves and many conflicting emotions. A kind, firm and understanding attitude will accomplish miracles.

16

Scenery

Much discussion takes place, mainly geared by the wish to save money, about the desirability of dispensing with scenery in amateur productions, and playing to curtains.

There are pockets of Theatre in the Round devotees in various parts of the country who are unanimous in declaring that scenery is not necessary. They argue that it distracts the attention of the audience. They say that a good play, well acted, should be strong enough to hold any audience.

I can appreciate this point of view, but I consider that few plays, however well acted, unless specially written for Theatre in the Round, could stand up to the stark nudity and untidiness of this form of theatre.

I am aware of the artistic and powerful effects one can evoke by subtle lighting, but the messy array of cables, spots and paraphernalia distracts me, as does the brushing of the actors who pass by my seat on their way to the central arena. I was irritated when I watched the television programme TW3. The whole thing was undisciplined, untidy and muddled. Further, however cleverly the lighting is arranged, when I am watching Theatre in the Round, I am aware throughout the performance of a row of eggheads sitting facing me. An actor's thigh, thrust in my sight line, can ruin my view.

I can see nothing to be sneered at in having an artistic setting, well-lit, with good grouping, within a frame, as a story is unfolded or a problem presented. The grimness of a kitchen sink is all very well, but there is beauty in life, and I cannot see why we should wallow in dustbins or sewers all the time.

The technological background of our modern world has a cold beauty and poetry of its own, but some of us are aware of other and more profound beauty. We value this warmer and more penetrating kind, and I consider we should put some of it into our drama. More important still, those of us who have a moral duty to the young should do anything we can to introduce beauty of every kind to the eager, vital, developing minds of our pupils.

Granted a person who can see beauty in a smoky chimney is a person whose acquaintance should be cultivated, but an individual who can enthuse about the beauty of a dewdrop on a rose, or a Chopin Nocturne, should not be despised.

It can be well imagined, having this attitude, that I was determined that we should strike a happy medium between no scenery and too much. Because I was dealing with young people who lived in smoky, drab surroundings, I felt it all the more imperative that we should bring light and colour into their lives. I wanted colourful scenery and costumes.

In our early shows we used curtains and simple mobile bits of scenery. They had to be small because we were working on school stages. It was a difficult task, as, with little or no proper lighting, I could not get the effects for which I was struggling. When we started to perform in other halls, the difficulties increased. One or two elder brothers and fathers offered to help. We then met and approached the problem in a businesslike manner. Our chief problem was that we had no place to construct the flats. After I had explained what a flat was—up to this point I think they were under the impression I was calling *them* names—one parent said he would be willing to loan his cellar for a workshop.

By now we were staging our shows at the Civic Theatre. This meant our flats had to be eleven feet high. To wean ourselves, we designed sets which were a combination of flats and curtains.

Our little group of enthusiasts set to work with a will. I was impressed and most thankful for their workmanlike attack. Their earnest desire to please, coupled with their cheerful sacrifice of time and effort, gave my flagging faith in humanity a facelift.

For three weeks they toiled in secrecy. Then they rang me to say they had finished the flats, and would like me to call and inspect them. They explained on the phone that they had had a most enjoyable time. Mistakes had caused amusement because of their childishness. Cuts and bruises had resulted from inexperience. Many cuss words had been used. Every evening that they had met to work had been rounded off with a little supper. Fish, chips, and Guinness had cemented friendship. Their wish was now that I should be satisfied.

Their attitude recalled to my mind the lines from *A Midsummer Night's Dream*:

> '*For never anything can be amiss*
> *When simpleness and duty tender it.*'

I made an appointment and duly turned up as arranged.

I was ushered down the cellar steps by a rather bashful parent. Fifteen narrow steps led down into their workshop. It was cramped, and lit by a single, stark light bulb. I could only marvel, as I glanced around, how five men had managed to make four flats, eleven foot by three in such a restricted area. The flats were well made, neatly covered with canvas and sized ready for painting.

With genuine feeling I complimented them on their industry. Their faces beamed with awkward satisfaction, shining palely in the wan light, as they stood around.

I glanced round, noting details. Then my heart gave a stab and plummeted into my boots.

There was one small, thickly cobwebbed window about eighteen inches square and one door smaller than the average door. These were the only outlets from the cellar. The door opened directly on to the steps which were at right-angles to the door. Facing the door was a wall. It was impossible to get the flats out of the cellar.

They saw me looking from the flats to the door. Then one burst out, ' 'Struth, how shall we get the damn things out?'

Then followed what the novelists term a pregnant silence. In those seconds many expressions remained unspoken. We just gazed at each other, speechless. Very feebly the youngest said, 'But, really, what are we going to do?'

There was only one thing we *could* do; dismantle the flats and get the pieces upstairs. We took off our jackets and set to work. I felt the heavy disappointment of the team myself and did all I could to boost their morale with what sounded to me hollow clichés.

After much exertion and straining numerous natural laws, we succeeded in getting the pieces upstairs. Somewhat mollified by the result, they reassembled the flats in the dining-room, whilst young members of the family looked on with amused expressions, but mercifully refrained from passing any comment. The finished result was not too neat, but nevertheless the flats were usable. We smiled when one of the team said, 'Weren't we fools? But we'll know better next time.' My heart jumped with relief. Evidently there was going to be another time. They were not going to resign.

This incident was the start of a staunch construction team which functioned for many years. Misfortune is frequently a stronger amalgam than success. We realized that if this group was to be a success, then we must have a fair-sized room where we could make and store flats. For the time being, another parent allowed us to store the scenery we now possessed in a room which at that time he was not using.

We advertised for a room, and inspected premises as we had done for a headquarters. I remember the aroma pervading one building we visited. We felt sure the owner had hidden a corpse under the floorboards.

I knew there was a good cellar under the Civic Theatre. I had an interview with the Chairman of the Buildings Committee and explained our needs, making it quite clear we were prepared to pay a rent for it. It would, I pointed out, be an ideal workshop for us. He assured me that our request would be considered.

Three weeks later we were told we could use the cellar

free of charge, if we observed certain conditions. These we very gratefully accepted and we are still making our scenery there. Although we have some public figures who have little good to say about us, we have other fair-minded and enlightened councillors who go out of their way to help us. To these friends we are deeply indebted, and we are humbly grateful to them for their keen and practical interest in our work.

Now the making of scenery is a messy business. All my helpers are voluntary workers, and not professional carpenters. Scenery under construction looks untidy. Some of the less friendly public figures, having no artistic leanings, look upon the work of the Theatre with a jaundiced eye. Complaints have been made against us, but, up to now, fair dealing has prevailed. Of course, many awkward situations would be avoided if we had a theatre of our own. We construct some of our smaller pieces of scenery at the Headquarters.

We have frequently had to simplify our sets more than I wished, because we have not sufficient helpers. Because we are not lucky enough to have an experienced carpenter in our ranks, we tend to take longer making our sets than we would if we could enlist more expert assistance. Certainly simple sets can be completely effective. But simplicity is not always easy, strange as this may seem.

Our Shakespearean sets are usually rearrangements of a very stark basic design. With a few interchangeable pieces and some cunning lighting, artistic, satisfying pictures can be arranged. Some moments, for instance, in our last production of *Julius Caesar* sent me into ecstacies (These stage folk are so gushing, aren't they?) I had 'Electrics' to thank for that. All we had on the stage were two pillars and some steps. They were painted just off-white. The lighting was excellent and we managed to achieve some of those effects which only seem to come our way once in the so-termed blue moon. No one who is disinterested in the art of production could ever really appreciate the great thrill a producer feels when the exact picture he has in his mind appears in every detail before him on the stage. When it does, then it is the result of complete sympathy between several people.

I have not as many helpers as I would like, but those I have are loyal. They do their utmost to help me put on our stage shows of which I am very proud. Without their assistance I would be helpless. I shall always be humbly grateful for this magnificent co-operation.

In costume plays, a simple neutral coloured background will ensure that the costumes show to the very best advantage.

Any set has to be planned with the stage on which it is to be erected in mind. Our stage at the Civic Theatre is small. The width of the proscenium arch is twenty-four feet. Wing space is practically non-existent. On stage left it is about six feet. Even this small space is cluttered up with the ropes controlling the barrels. On stage right the large lighting kit takes up all the space.

From the floats to the cyclorama is thirteen feet. Behind the cyclorama there is a passage two feet wide. There is one entrance on to the stage, up stage right. We cannot fly any scenery at all. To the uninitiated this means that we cannot by means of ropes and pulleys draw any flats up vertically out of sight nor lower other flats. This can be done in properly equipped theatres and enables whole scenes to be changed in the matter of seconds.

Long scene changes can ruin a play. In our early, inexperienced days we transgressed in this direction. This fault has been ironed out. The Stage Manager should always rehearse his scene changes as carefully as the producer rehearses the cast. When I am preparing my Prompt Book, I make detailed notes of scenic intricacies, and discuss these fully with my Stage Manager.

All stage staff should wear rubber-soled shoes. Each member should be given specific tasks, scene by scene, and should never deviate from the scheduled procedure, once it has been decided on by the Stage Manager. No casual, slipshod attitude should be tolerated. One careless, disinterested member could easily ruin the show. A clumsy, sullen stage staff can undo in one performance all the work a producer has put in over weeks. This is no exaggeration. A word of advice. Do not despise female stage staff, they can be good.

Powder colours for scenery painting should be ordered from a shade card if you cannot visit the suppliers in person. Always use a colour about two shades darker than you visualize for your set. Lighting takes out some of the intensity of the colour. I like to use oil-bound poster paint for bold designs. It is bright and comes up well under the lighting. Powder colours must be mixed with size or the colours will flake off, with disastrous results to costumes.

I like to sketch out a rough of the design, and discuss colours with the stage manager and the lighting expert. This saves time because I can do my proper sketch right away. A model of the set built to scale and coloured should be made. This gives the Stage Manager an opportunity to point out any snags before his staff starts to construct the scenery. I like to see the Stage Manager once every week to find out how things are progressing.

Any member who has a leaning towards art can generally be found a job in the scenic department. Given guidance, time and a little money, a spot of elaborate scenery should not prove too much for a youth theatre. It is jolly to have a splash with something a little less austere sometimes. Certainly in this department of a theatre one sees clearly the results of effort. That is good for the soul.

17

Wardrobe

From my earliest days I was fascinated by dressing up. Often, as I played in the gardens and woods around 'Oaklands', by means of odd bits of clothing, borrowed hats, and sundry props, I was Jim Hawkins, a Wise Man or the leader of a spy ring—whatever the whim of the moment demanded. I was a lonely figure, but the realm of my imagination was packed with heroes and rogues, all of whom became my daily companions.

I remember, on the occasion of the coronation of George V and Queen Mary, the pageantry as depicted in the pages of the *Illustrated London News* fired the tinder of my fertile mind. When autumn came, I recall vividly how I made myself a herald's surcoat of conkers in what must have been an ingenious way, because it was a huge success. I stalked through the woods leading an imaginary procession of kings, dukes, earls and foreign potentates.

When I started producing, I hankered after lavish period costumes rich with braid and made of sumptuous velvets and brocades. Motley's magnificent costumes and décor for Gielgud's production of *Romeo and Juliet* stunned me. Our drab, welfare state has given the people a dreary utilitarian outlook. Pageantry and ceremony have been eclipsed, and our lives are all the duller for it. Our young people yearn for colourful costumes and unusual styles. And why not, provided cleanliness is observed?

As I began to produce plays in school, my wife and I found ourselves designing and adapting costumes, using the most unlikely materials. We made armour, surcoats, headgear and accessories. The results were surprisingly successful. The boys wearing these bizarre and colourful creations experienced an exhilaration which caused them to grow as we watched them. They were stimulated and benefited enormously.

Our lack of money strangled at birth my ideas of lavish costumes. The shows were planned so we could use easily contrived costumes. We added a few from our school wardrobe. The parents were co-operative, but I realized that if my dreams of exotic costumes were to materialize, then a fair amount of any money we made would have to be diverted to the Wardrobe. Once we could establish a nucleus of good costumes we would add to the stock bit by bit until we would achieve my aim.

After we had been going about three years, a parent called to see me. She was Mrs Hilda Donigan, a genial rosy-faced woman with the most beautiful blue eyes. In them shone a smile of such kindliness as is seldom seen and a piquant Irish humour. Her younger son was our comedy lead, one of the most brilliant natural comics I have ever seen. Mrs Donigan had been to see our shows, and felt we deserved better costumes. She told me she was a dressmaker and offered to take charge of our Wardrobe. I accepted the offer with alacrity, and thus began one of the happiest associations we have had in the Theatre. Hilda was not only our Wardrobe Mistress, but our loyal and trusted friend. Never once did I see her angry. In the midst of the chaos of making seventy costumes for *The Gondoliers*, or swamped by the intricacies of a Shakespearean production, her smile, her wit and her perpetual good nature were an example to us all. For fifteen years she was in charge of our Costume Department, and then came tragedy. She was out shopping, preparing for the christening of her youngest grandchild, when she was knocked down by a speed-merchant, and died a few hours later.

I do not believe in stressing the sadness of life to the young. Nevertheless we cannot dodge sorrow; it just has to be faced. I have never witnessed a more poignant scene than Hilda's funeral. Many of our young members were there, carrying pathetic little posies, which they reverently placed by the graveside. Their tears testified to the love they had for their friend.

Hilda's memory is kept alive by the presentation each year of the Hilda Donigan Shield. It is presented at the end of each season to the girl who has given the outstanding performance of the year. The winner holds it for one year.

Hilda's passing left us stunned. We just did not know where to look for her successor. As we sat wondering what to do, we remembered how Hilda's scissors would flash as she chatted and laughed with us. The electric sewing machine would whirr, and as we talked, in a matter of minutes, another dress would be added to the pile waiting for someone to put the buttons on.

Then, once again, help appeared out of the blue. My phone rang. It was Mrs Veale, Betty to us. She had helped on the Wardrobe Committee for a time but family duties had compelled her to resign. She now offered to take over Hilda's job. She has proved a gem. With her group of helpers she does a magnificent job.

Over the years we have amassed a truly amazing set of costumes. When it is all in the cupboards and on the racks, we could number something in the region of fifteen hundred costumes, or maybe more. Only very occasionally have we had to hire a costume. The other autumn when we did *Twelfth Night* the only thing we hired was Sir Andrew Aguecheek's wig.

Following my broadcast of July, 1964, we received some very welcome additions to our Wardrobe. One lady who had been a missionary in Durban sent us a magnificent Indian shawl. Another, over eighty years of age, sent us her wedding dress. It is a beautiful white satin dress, entirely made and embroidered by hand. We took a photograph of one of our girls wearing it and sent a print to the donor. We were thrilled by the interest and generosity of these unknown friends.

When we have decided to do a costume play, I have several meetings with the Wardrobe Department. Books are taken out of the Library and pored over. Photographs and drawings are closely scrutinized. Sketches are made, colours and designs are decided upon, and the Wardrobe personnel set to work.

Accessories such as purses, handbags, articles of jewellery and even gloves may have to be made. These things are most important as they enhance the effect of the costumes.

The members of our Wardrobe Department are clever at adapting existing costumes. This is useful, and saves us money. The co-operative effort involved is the most valuable angle of our work. All who help look at the finished production and feel they had a hand in it, which has a beneficial effect on an individual.

When we have finally decided on the costume scheme, the cast is measured and fitted. As a costume is finished the person who has to wear it is carefully fitted again, and any alterations necessary are made.

Many groups fight shy of costume plays on the score of expense, or the difficulty of making costumes. It has been my experience that most of the things I have wished to do in my life have been either expensive or difficult. Frequently both. Because of the difficulty I have been all the more determined to do them. Often under pressure my inventive faculties have been stimulated, and the results have been amazing and exhilarating. We should tackle things and not stand aside and moan 'It can't be done.' Life without challenge would be savourless.

In musicals and Shakespearean productions we usually call a specific 'Dress' rehearsal. We can, on such an occasion, leisurely and carefully check costume details. The cast has an opportunity to wear the dresses and get the feel of them. It is essential that a period costume is well and truly 'worn'. To do this adds to the standard of the performance and the actor is more comfortable on the stage.

The purchase of material for our Wardrobe has always

been an expensive item on our budget. Perhaps from an over-sensitive pride, we have done little in the way of asking for donations of material. However, when we were preparing *Richard III*, I wrote to three of the largest Manchester firms, explaining who and what we were. I politely asked if they would be willing to donate any scraps of material. I was most gratified when we received pleasant letters from each firm together with some pieces of very beautiful material. They were a generous size and with attractive colours and designs. Some of the clubs and groups of people to whom I have lectured about the Theatre have also given us material which has been of great use to us.

When Mrs Donigan was in charge of the Wardrobe we started a Hire Service. This we did for two reasons. We wished to help struggling societies, and in the process hoped to make a little money. We have built up a clientele of satisfied customers since the scheme was introduced. For a time we were willing to loan to any school in our district any costumes we could supply, free of charge, if they would guarantee to bring a party of at least twenty to the next production. Such is the frailty of human nature that we found the promises were made, but after a time they were not very well kept, so we had to withdraw the offer. We were a little sad about this because we really tried to be helpful. On one occasion a school wanted to borrow some costumes, but said they did not think they could raise a party to see the show. We suggested they took the costumes and sent us a donation. They took about twenty costumes. At the end of nine weeks we rang up and pointed out that other schools were wanting the same costumes. To get our goods we had to send one of the Committee with his car to collect them, and the Head sent a letter containing a donation—half a crown.

After many and varied experiences equally surprising, we decided to make a specific charge for each costume. We fixed on five shillings per costume. This modest sum has meant we have helped groups, and at the same time brought a smile to the face of our Treasurer.

This scheme is in the hands of the Wardrobe Mistress and anyone interested in The Service should write to her:

The Wardrobe Mistress,
Stretford Children's Theatre,
28 Talbot Road,
Old Trafford,
Manchester, 16.

Please enclose a stamped addressed envelope, and I beg you to give us as much notice as possible. All our helpers are voluntary workers, many with full-time jobs. Furthermore we have to prepare costumes for our own productions.

One last word. If we should be able to help you, PLEASE RETURN THE COSTUMES PROMPTLY, and so enable us to help as many as possible.

18

Properties

This department of our activities is very popular with our boys. They find plenty of opportunity to try out their inventive faculties, often with surprising results. Some of our non-acting members find a niche here that gives them the chance to feel one of the busy crowd.

We frequently find the most amazing inventive talent possessed by the quiet little girl whom we have tried very hard to interest in many things, or the shy boy who never volunteers to read a part in a play yet never misses a rehearsal.

I am green with envy when I walk through the painting, sculpture, stage-designing rooms at the Cannon Hill Park Centre in Birmingham. This set-up is what I have always visualized. It is wonderful to realize that at last we are awakening to the fact that we must have places where we can feed the artistic hunger of thousands of young people all over the country. We have struggled to do just this in our small way for twenty-one years. In the matter of having a home of our own we are much better off than many groups.

Our Props Department is an absorbing part of our work. Every show we do demands something which we cannot borrow or afford to buy, so we must make. Here is yet another challenge.

The boys are always keen to make armour, guns, banners and the more flamboyant articles. Time spent decorating a shield is amply justified when one sees the effect on the night. The girls turn out some very charming costume accessories.

Props for each show are put under the care of a Property Mistress, who may have some assistants. We find that the girls are a little more reliable in this position than the boys.

Once the play is chosen, the Property Mistress makes out a list of the props, scene by scene, I make out a similar list, and then we cross-check. Then the list is carefully set down. There are columns for each performance and before the curtain goes up each night, every single item on the list is checked. We usually have them on a table off stage right.

Properties required stage left are carefully placed on a table off left, and an assistant placed in charge. Hand props are given out to the individuals requiring them, and when they leave the stage, or at the end of the act, they return them to the Property Mistress. When the lists are checked, we generally mark all those items we can borrow or buy. Arrangements are made for collecting them and details of where we are loaning them from are entered in a note-book.

The common experience in the amateur stage world is that societies are very ready to borrow properties, but are very slack at returning them. This casual attitude gives a society a bad name and people are reluctant to loan props. Borrowed properties should be returned at the earliest possible moment after the last performance.

Certain props will not be available until the actual performance, or perhaps the dress rehearsal. Substitute props should be used in rehearsal. I like props or their substitutes to be used in rehearsal at least a month before the show.

If drinks are necessary, or more particularly if a full meal has to be manœuvred, you cannot have the props too early. To leave them to the last minute is asking for a disaster on the opening night.

There is nothing worse than the clumsy handling of props. It spoils the flow of the action and ruins the picture. A word here about drinking on stage. Some people argue that mimed drinking is correct. They say one should use the imagination. I am quite prepared to use my imagination on something really important and significant, but not on a simple action like drinking. I like to see actual fluid in the cup or goblet. Also, if the liquid is supposed to be hot, let me see the steam rising as the cup of tea is poured out.

At this point we carefully prepare a list of all the props we are going to make. Volunteers are invited and teams are set to work on various articles. It may be necessary to do quite a bit of research in the library. Sketches have to be made. Discussions as to size take place. Careful measurements are taken. Sometimes a large number of youngsters are busy on a few props.

Needless to say, these things must not be left till last. Everything should be prepared at the earliest moment.

We use every conceivable material in making our props. No one's scrap box or junk corner is safe. It is fascinating to try out new materials. Many of our elaborate props cost us nothing except the time spent making them.

In our *Richard III* we had some effective crowns. They were made of cardboard carefully constructed, strengthened and painted. The cardboard was cut from boxes which had contained our gas fires when they were delivered to the headquarters. A few inventive minds can save the Theatre pounds.

I think it would be most helpful to name a few of the props we have made for some of our productions and explain how we have made them. I do not claim our way is the best but at any rate it has proved a workable way to us, so may well be for others.

The basic requirements for property-making are: pencil, cardboard, ruler, scissors, needles, thread, a good adhesive— we use Bostik—various-sized paint brushes, paint—our choice is oil-bound poster paint—and of course gold and silver paint.

Apart from any kind of cardboard, we always carry a good stock of a very thin, tough cardboard, called Elephantide. This is obtainable in rolls of varying widths, or pieces. It is supplied by:

B. S. & W. Whiteley, Ltd,
Papermakers,
Poole-in-Wharfedale,
Yorkshire.

A modern product which has proved excellent for the making of scenery and props is Jablite expanded polystyrene. It is excellent for masonry, rocks, sculpture effects and such props as panels and unusually shaped articles. It can be quickly and easily carved, and is very light in weight. Jablite is manufactured and marketed by:

Jablo Group Sales Ltd,
Mill Lane,
Waddon,
Croydon,
Surrey.

A whole book could be written about making props. I propose to illustrate how we make some of our more interesting properties by sketches.

Figure 1. **Breastplates**

A The basis of this form of breastplate is the papier-mâché tray used to pack eggs. We usually make each of our breastplates to measure. Having decided on the size, we adjust the trays by overlapping and sticking with Bostik.

The hollows on the side that we have chosen to be the back are filled with plaster of Paris mixed into a thick paste. Then over the entire back we stick canvas or a piece of material, e.g. an unpicked coat. The edges are bound with strips of leather. Shoulder straps of leather are added. The projections at the bottom are pieces of Elephantide bordered with leather or thick cardboard.

The back is made in the same way if one is required. Of course, if a cloak is to be worn, no back plate is necessary. We usually incorporate a belt under the breastplate, arrang-

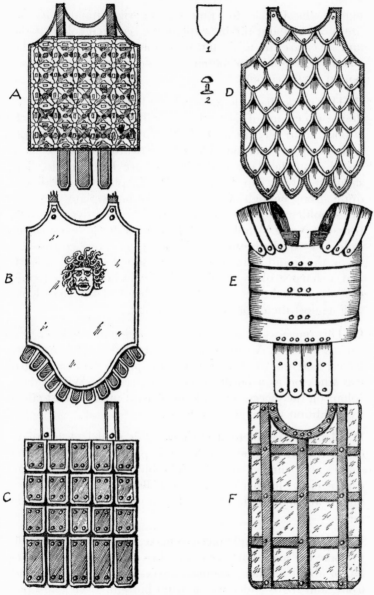

K   Figure 1. BREASTPLATES

ing for the buckle to come on the right-hand side. To finish off we paint the breastplate the required colour. Gold and silver are the most suitable colours, but, if a particular colour is required to match a colour scheme, we use oil-bound poster colours.

B This model has a foundation of Elephantide. The centre design is cut out of fairly thick cardboard and stuck on. It is possible to buy, at a Do It Yourself store, plastic motifs which can be stuck on. The edge is leather or thick cardboard, and the flaps at the bottom are Elephantide. The shoulder straps can be leather or Elephantide, which is quite strong enough. In most of these breastplates we rivet the shoulder straps on. We use round-headed rivets as illustrated at No. 2. A hole is punched through the two surfaces to be riveted, the bottom part of the rivet is pushed through them, the round head placed on the top of the bottom part, and a sharp stroke with a hammer will make a very strong fastening. Furthermore the shining head of the rivet looks well against the colour of the breastplate.

C This one was made of pieces of linoleum, stuck on to a canvas backing. A small space was left between each piece. Rivets were put at each corner of the pieces, and cardboard was stuck on as a border round each section. With a dark colour on the pieces, and gold borders, it made a most effective addition to the general décor.

D Elephantide cut to shape forms this model. A template of cardboard as shown at No. 1 is prepared and then the shapes are pencilled round it. The binding around the edge can be either leather or cardboard. Rivets (as in No. 2) are placed at each point. The result is a most effective costume piece.

E This is a very simple piece to make. Strips of Elephantide to make the main part are cut and riveted through an overlap of about an inch. Shoulder pieces are riveted back and front, and strips added at the front bottom. Eyelets are put at the back and then, when worn, the breastplate will be laced on.

F A piece of canvas or coarse material forms the basis of this. Strips of leather about an inch and a quarter wide are riveted on, and the whole is bound by a strip of leather. The leather strips and binding can be gilded, and if the background is a dark colour, the effect is striking.

Figure 2. **Banners**

A We use every kind of material imaginable for these. **A** was made of hardboard, with a background painted gold. The strips, cut from hardboard and glued on, were painted crimson.

B A frame of hardboard was put around a piece of green silk (an old dance dress) on both sides of a backing of canvas. A piece of gold fringe from a lampshade was put along the bottom, and strips of dark green webbing hung the whole from the bar, which was an old stair rod. The motif was cut out of purple felt, and stuck on with Bateman's rubber adhesive.

C This could be either stiff or flexible. Hardboard with passe-partout border, and cardboard motifs stuck on, would provide a rigid form. Velvet (both sides) with motifs and border stitched on or stuck on would provide a small banner which would fall in effective folds.

D Old architect's drawings were boiled and the linen stitched together and left white. Coloured tape was stitched around the edges, and the whole backed with canvas. An old curtain tassel was added, and a loop of tape stitched behind at the point so that the holder could slip his thumb through it and so hold the whole banner steady.

E Hardboard painted the same each side made this for a production of *The Mikado*.

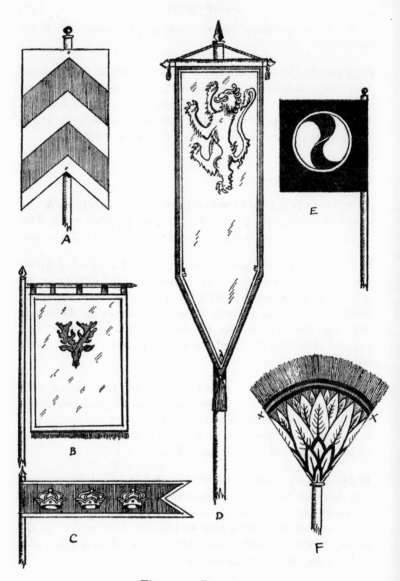

Figure 2. BANNERS

F A Biblical play called for this design. Two pieces of cardboard, shaped up to **XX**, are stuck together, and painted the same each side. The fringed top is made of Denison's crêpe paper. It was stuck between the two layers of cardboard for about an inch. The pole extended to the top of the cardboard.

Figure 3. **Crowns**

All crowns start as a simple coronet as shown at **A**. We make this from Elephantide. It is possible to purchase by the yard, at a very reasonable cost, plastic borders with a design in high relief. These circlets make most effective accessories in the wardrobe.

D We usually make the main circle of two or three thicknesses of cardboard. In this model the points were made of two thicknesses stuck between two other layers of plain band. The small decoration at each point was a long scarf pin with a coloured head. Rivets were placed at intervals around.

E This is fundamentally the same. The trefoils were built up on pieces of wire inserted between the layers of cardboard. Six layers were used, and strips of webbing were glued in between.

F This looks elaborate, but it is not so difficult to make as it appears. Layers of cardboard form the basis and in between the middle layers is a strip of metal. The leaf design is painted on Elephantide, and stuck on a second layer to give it strength. Both this model and **E** model have cord stuck around the edge, and gilded. The jewels around the base are painted peas and clear gum sweets stuck in the appropriate places. Small pearls from old necklaecs are used when available.

G Again this is not difficult to make. Layers of card board strengthened with metal strips which came round our

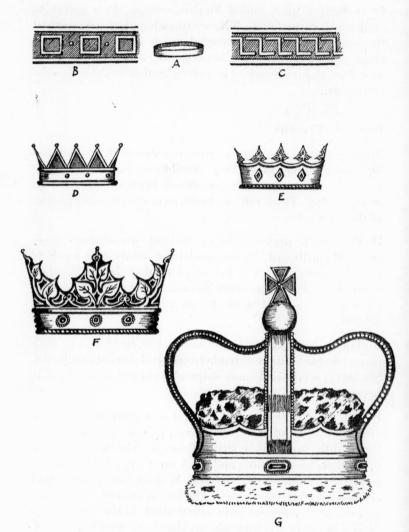

Figure 3. CROWNS

Elephantide order made the big loops. Pearls were stuck around the loops. The orb was a table tennis ball with a cardboard cross. A cake frill stuck around the bottom, with ermine marks painted on, and red velvet cap complete the effect.

Figure 4. **Goblets**

We use as the bases of most of our goblets the plastic containers and picnic drinking cups which are easily obtainable. To make the stems cotton bobbins **B** are used. Two of them are joined by inserting a dowel rod in the central hole. The rod is coated with Bostik before insertion. The diagram **C** illustrates this method. The plastic container is stuck on the top, and a circle of cardboard, or, better still, three-ply wood is stuck on the bottom.

A more elaborate stem can be turned out of wood **E** and stuck on the base of the container, as shown at **D**. The finished goblet can be painted in plain gold or silver, or indeed any desired colour. To make a much richer effect, a design is cut out of cardboard, and stuck round the goblet, as shown in diagram **D**. If such a design is then painted with gold or silver, it gives a chased appearance. Plastic d'oyleys have designs on them which can be cut out and used in this manner.

A goblet painted in deep red, and with a design cut out in cardboard, as shown at **F**, painted in gold and stuck on, becomes a most decorative property. To cut out such a pattern, use an X-Acto knife.

Figure 5. **Helmets**

Although the crowns of discarded hats can be used as the foundations of helmets, I prefer to build them up with Elephantide and paper.

The preliminary strips are laid across the head and fastened to the band going round the head, as shown in

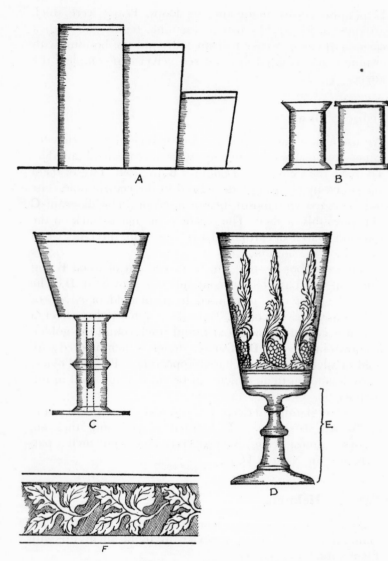

Figure 4. GOBLETS

diagrams **A** and **B**. To make the helmet **C** it is only necessary to stick on shaped pieces of thin cardboard. Each piece overlaps and is stuck with Bostik.

Elephantide is the basic material for all the helmets illustrated here. For the Roman type shown **D** a strip is shaped as at **X**, and two pieces as at **E**, and three small pieces for the neck shield. They are all riveted to the crown. Suitably painted gold or silver, with design in black, it successfully simulates the Roman style.

Design **F** has a visor made of two pieces fastened together, and a chin piece in one piece. They are both riveted to the crown. The collar can be quite separate. Three pieces are measured and cut in strips. They are riveted to strips shown by the dotted lines.

Model **G**, plan at **H**, is made of six pieces. They overlap about three-quarters of an inch and are riveted. The front two sections are made by two pieces riveted above the eyes, and two to cover the cheeks, riveted to the side pieces.

The Cromwellian style is made of sections riveted together. Ear and neck pieces are riveted to the crown. Wire forms the mask and is fixed to a wire which passes round the head, fixed just inside the crown.

The Trojan helmet is very effective, but not difficult to make. The mask is one shaped piece riveted at the sides, and three pieces form the neck shield. The crest is made in a triangular form and shaped as in the diagram. The front view is shown at **K**. Red crêpe paper, about six inches deep, is folded as the dark line in diagram **L**. It is stuck inside the cardboard crest for about an inch. The projecting paper is then cut to simulate feathers or hair, and shaped to a point at **Z**. The whole crest is riveted to the crown as shown in diagram **J**. Painted gold, with shaded parts in a dark colour, it plays its part on the set with distinction.

For the comfort of the wearer it is a good idea for all crowns and helmets to have a strip of foam rubber stuck round the headband. Allowance for this should be made when measurements are being taken.

Figure 5. HELMETS

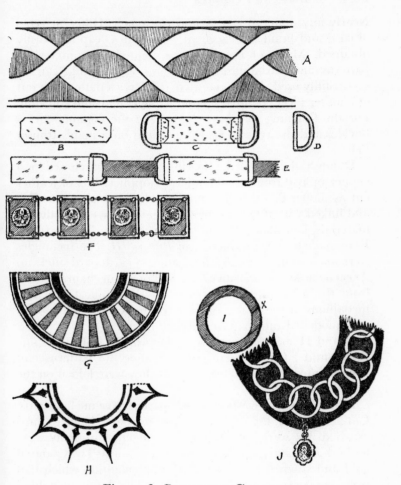

Figure 6. BELTS AND COLLARS

Figure 6. **Belts and Collars**

Nearly any material can be used as a belt. Different types of cord and braid are excellent, and both cheap and easily obtained. Many of them can be plaited into interesting patterns and variations. Once again Elephantide can be successfully used. **A**, strip painted, can have a pattern cut out of another piece, painted a contrasting colour and stuck on. For the fastening for our belts we use the common tie, a buckle, and the type of fastening found on a man's trouser belt.

D shows what is called a 'D' ring. It can be purchased for a copper or two from any handicraft supplier. Bits of leather cut as shown **B**, stitched around the D ring—shown at **C**— and linked with different coloured leather, or even different materials, can make the most attractive belt. The example **F** we made for our production of *Richard III*. The rectangles were made of linoleum, having frames of cardboard stuck on. At each corner we fixed an eyelet, and pieces of chain salvaged from the girls' junk boxes supplied the connections. The medallions in the centre of each rectangle were milk bottle tops modelled into patterns and stuck on.

G and **H** show examples of collars made from the same Elephantide. Circles were cut and after the patterns had been painted and the centre cut out they were folded on the dotted line.

I shows a plastic washer. A kind parent gave me hundreds. Cut across at **X**, the washer retained its shape, being as hard as wood. We were able to link them together in many ways for both belts and ceremonial chains. The one at **J** was painted gold and stitched on to a collar of Elephantide which had been covered with crimson velvet. The large medallion was the trade mark cut off a roll of material, and stuck on cardboard.

19

Lighting and Sound Effects

To achieve a first-class production, scenery may not be essential, but your actors must be visible. You must illuminate your cast. One could manage an entertainment using sound alone, as in ordinary sound radio, but to increase the concept of action, it is necessary to see what is happening.

I would say that subtle lighting improves the impact of any type of play. Poor, brash, unconsidered lighting can ruin any production.

Personally, I am very keen in certain types of play, Shakespeare for instance, to arrange the lighting so that shadows play a powerful part in building up a mood. May I say, that to do this, it is not necessary to have a very elaborate lighting system. Whatever the extent of your lighting kit, it depends how you use it. An hour's experimenting will be time well-spent, and you will be amazed at the extra punch you will get out of lines you thought trite.

If the lighting is very well thought out, I am prepared to watch Theatre in the Round. This type of Theatre *must* have very subtle lighting.

I always try to work out my lighting plot so that costumes and sets are enhanced by the subtlety of the lighting.

My lighting expert, John Evans, has been working with me for many years, and there is a real rapport between us. He knows instinctively the effect I want, and has got so accustomed to my ideas that he frequently guesses what lighting arrangements I am likely to ask for. When one has such a co-operative partner it makes one rather lazy.

I discuss with John, as soon as rehearsals start, the

possibilities of a scene. I tell him what I would like. Occasionally I ask for more than our outfit can give. Then I have to modify my ideas. This happens very seldom, because John will move the heavens to give me my lighting. I have known him stay up nearly all night to make most intricate alterations so that I chortle with glee.

One should write out a full lighting plot. But, as I have said, I get rather lazy. John has a script of the play. I have that preliminary chat with him, and then, unless some unexpected snag occurs, I do not see John until perhaps three weeks before the show.

We then meet, often at my house, and go through the script with a small-tooth comb. Any changes I may have decided on, I most meticulously explain. Then I do not see John until the Sunday before the dress rehearsal. The rest is the actual rehearsal, when we rehearse all we decided at our interviews.

The best-known name in stage lighting is Strand Electric.

Another well-known firm is Furse, of Nottingham. This firm supplied the lighting installation in the Stretford Civic Theatre. It is their 'Deliclour' System. The great advantage of this system is that, by mechanical selection, an unskilled operator can succeed in getting colour changes of great subtlety.

We have three lighting battens in sets of four: white, red, green and blue. Our footlights—which we seldom use—are in the same sets as the battens. On our number one batten, that is, the batten nearest the proscenium arch, there are two 1,000-watt soft focus spots. There are four similar spots, F.O.H. (This means front of house, or in the auditorium.) They can be adjusted to cover any given acting areas on the stage.

We also have three 1,000-watt wing floods. In addition there is a 1,000-watt cloud projector. This is a large circular slide with clouds on it that passes in front of a lens. The slide is focused on to the cyclorama. A clockwork motor makes the slide turn and the result is a very striking lighting effect.

We have a twenty-four-foot ground row. This is really a batten again in sets of four, resting on the floor and allowing the light to be directed upwards on to the cyclorama or part of the scenery. It is effective, but takes up too much space.

I am fully aware that our lighting system, though efficient, is far from up to date. Nevertheless it is all we have. I dream of the barrels of spots and all the latest equipment. It is no surprise, surely, that I long for a theatre of our own, fitted out with all these items. Well, maybe a miracle will happen.

As John is a recording expert, he is also in charge of sound effects. This embraces a very wide range of possibilities, from the sound of water dripping in a cave to The Last Post. Seldom is the effects department at a loss. We have had some weird assignments to get the sound we wanted.

Realistic effects are much easier to obtain these days through the medium of the tape recorder. There are on the market quite a number of records of all kinds of sounds. These are very handy, but continuing our policy of doing as much as we can ourselves, we prefer to record the actual sounds whenever we possibly can. The availability of a portable tape recorder, run off batteries, makes this hunt a real lark.

When we did *A Man Dies* we wanted the bugle call of The Last Post. We approached the Commanding Officer of one of the Manchester Territorial units, and he most willingly agreed to co-operate. We went along to the barracks, and much care was taken to ensure that we had a perfect recording. I may add that we all had a very pleasant evening. The buglers were invited to a performance to hear their contribution to the show.

In 1964 I wanted the sound effects to be particularly good for our *Richard III*. I asked for chanting in the background when the corpse of Henry VI was carried in, and a Te Deum in the scene of Richard's coronation. I rang up the Canon in charge of the large Roman Catholic church, St Ann's. I had never met the Canon but I explained what I required. Most courteously he arranged for me to have a chat with his choirmaster.

I found the latter a most charming, co-operative person, anxious to supply just what I wanted. He actually composed a Te Deum in the correct musical idiom of the period, and this, together with the chanting I wanted, was recorded in the church and the tape sent to me.

Only a keen producer will understand what such kind co-operation means. It is invaluable, and I am deeply grateful for such kindness. Music is of great help in creating a mood. I am well aware it can be overdone. Once again, a little careful planning is needed.

A word about interval music. It is necessary to be most careful in the choice of interval records. Frequently one hears the most unsuitable music played—both at the interval, and before and after the show. If a musical expert is not on hand to advise on this matter, the nearest college of music would no doubt be willing to advise.

Sometimes owing to poor acoustics, certain effects do not record well. On the other hand it might be because of the particular tape recorder. We find that, however careful we have been, wind or storm sounds tend to sound confused. We have made a wind machine which, together with a thunder sheet, we operate when we need any sound of stormy weather.

Whoever is to do the effects, make sure it is a reliable person. Being able to record all or most of your effects on one tape in the correct order means that one person can operate it. Your effects man should be thoroughly conversant with every detail of the play. We do our best to see that all sound effects are ready at least three weeks before the show. The person responsible should attend rehearsals from a very early date, at least once a week, so that he can get the feel of the exact timing.

It is no exaggeration to say that an ill-timed cough, bell,

or strain of music could wreck in one second, a scene which has been building up to a strong climax. Your effects man *must* be reliable. The second 'Effects' starts treating his job in a casual manner, sack him.

20

Make-up

A few days after our first show, I met a dear old lady who was full of praise for our efforts. She explained to me how she had enjoyed the performance. She had only one criticism. In the gravest of tones she said she was very surprised I had allowed the youngsters to use make-up.

There are times when silence is the best answer.

In small school halls with little or no stage lighting, it would be wrong to use full stage make-up, but, of course, if you are using battens, floods, spots and all the paraphernalia of correct stage lighting, then make-up is essential.

The ideal way in any dramatic group is that each artist in a cast should be responsible for his own make-up. Each should gradually build up his own make-up box. As today's prices for greasepaint and all the accessories of this art have rocketed, this can be a costly affair. However, one or two, from time to time, do make the effort. We do have a communal make-up box. Actually it is an old-fashioned travelling case, which was given to the Theatre some years ago.

Three or four of our older members are responsible for the make-up, under the eagle eye of Hazel who has been a member of the Theatre for some twelve years. In each production there is usually one of the cast who knows enough about make-up to help the group. A few can make themselves up, if it is a straight make-up. It is a fairly difficult task to make a fifteen-year-old look forty. It is easier to make him look eighty.

Hazel reads the script and makes notes. Shortly I give her a list of characters with make-up particulars of each. There is a special note on moustaches, beards and any special character requirements. A note of the wigs we require is made. It is very important that these are ordered early. Arrangements have to be made for them to be fitted, collected and returned. If Hazel has any queries, she contacts me and we discuss them. She briefs her group and they plan their *modus operandi*.

When we have a large cast, as in a musical or a Shakespeare, a few extra casual helpers are enlisted from the non-acting members. They are shown how to put on foundation and straight make-up. We may have one person putting on foundation, another eye shadow, a third lining and so on.

The art of make-up repays careful study and experiment. Careless make-up I find is the main fault with many amateur groups I meet when I adjudicate. This has always surprised me. As the female of the species has brought daily make-up to such a high standard, I would have thought those girls would have excelled in this department. But here, as elsewhere, the female is completely unpredictable.

When giving my summing-up remarks at adjudications, I frequently make a suggestion. It is that two or three groups have a whip-round and jointly engage an expert in make-up to instruct them in the rudiments of make-up. They could then take this information back to their respective groups, and start experimenting. I am often asked which make-up we use: we have always favoured Leichner's items.

21

The Actual Show

For several years we have kept to the same pattern as regards the week of production. We rent the Civic Theatre for a week, from Sunday to Saturday. This week is always a thrilling time for everyone concerned with the production. For myself the thrill has never diminished throughout the years. It is exhilarating and completely absorbing. As I am dealing with young people, it is a thousandfold more rewarding and exciting.

Usually, on the Sunday morning, the stage staff assembles at the Civic Theatre around 10.30. As they have been busy during the previous six or eight weeks making the scenery in the cellar, it is more or less ready to be brought up on to the stage. As with all theatrical groups, there are always a few last-minute completions and alterations to be made. The ingenuity of my stage staff is a wonder to behold. Truly, necessity is the mother of invention.

I never understand why public buildings have to have so many awkward corners. Although we make our scenery in the most convenient sizes, it is a difficult job to bring the pieces up from the cellar on to the stage.

We try to get the help of a few extra hands as young lads cannot safely handle the heavier pieces on their own, however willing they may be. A father or older brother is shanghaied into service. Quite a few non-acting girls help in this department.

Other members call at the Headquarters and collect the props and the skips containing the costumes. Again, a kind father with a van is often talked into giving up his

Sunday morning lay-in to help. If we cannot arrange it this way, then a carter is engaged. The props and costumes have been packed the previous Friday evening.

The set is erected, costumes checked and props put out in readiness for the dress rehearsal. Costumes are hung on the racks in the dressing room ready for the Wardrobe staff who come down later in the day when a mass pressing and last-minute fitting and altering takes place.

'Electrics' checks his lighting particulars, sound equipment and interval music. He edits his recordings and rehearses with his assistants, if any. If there is a larger number of sound effects than usual, then he may have two or three extra helpers. This Sunday morning may be the first time the sound effects have been fully rehearsed, owing to unforeseen difficulties. As it is most important these should be timed to the second, they must have careful rehearsal. Many of them of course will have been rehearsed for several weeks.

At the side, on stage right, is a small recess. In this we have a table for properties where all props are placed in readiness. The Property Mistress or her assistants check the various articles and they are carefully put on this table in the most convenient position for being picked up. Any props required on stage left are put on a small table on the left in the same way.

On the Sunday there is usually a rehearsal in the large dressing room at 2 o'clock. This continues without a break other than for a cup of tea until 5 o'clock. This is an important occasion. Absence except for illness is serious. I do not like to encroach on members' time at the week-ends unless things are going badly. This is the only week-end rehearsal. We call it Preparation Sunday. Usually it is a good rehearsal; it breaks the ice for the dress rehearsal and is particularly useful to members who have not played in the Civic Theatre before. We show them the layout and carefully explain the rules and regulations covering the actual production.

Hazel calls to have a last-minute chat about any make-up queries she may have. We may have some last sudden inspirations about improving particular characters. Such co-operation is a great relief to me.

During the day I make it my duty to have a chat with a representative from each department of the Theatre to discuss last-minute alterations which have to be effected, or minor difficulties which crop up, and give a word of encouragement here and there, especially to the 'Freshers'.

On this Sunday there is a tangible sense of occasion. There is the feeling of 'where two or three are gathered together' in a common aim. This generates strength and power. Now the cast realizes the great day is near, I can feel the keen desire of the team to do its utmost.

Sometimes I may feel just a little depressed about the standard at this rehearsal. Occasionally a newcomer perhaps has not been serious enough in his efforts and there is a visible weakness in his performance compared with the rest of the cast. Whilst not making any member of the cast feel inadequate to the responsibility of the task ahead, I very tactfully, maybe privately, point out this shortcoming, and express the hope that it will be better at the dress rehearsal. This is usually enough to ensure a real response. I always put myself out to help any individual with personal difficulties. It is this feeling that we all belong to one family which has enabled us to do such productions as we have.

As we have such a very impressive lighting kit, this always intrigues the new members of the cast. To minimize the effects of this attraction at the dress rehearsal, on this Sunday I usually get 'Electrics' to demonstrate to the 'Freshers' what can be done with the switchboard. The looks on their faces as the rainbow hues change at the touch of a switch are a picture to see. Because of this exhibition, there are fewer gaping mouths at the Monday rehearsal.

I make a special point of having a chat with Prompt. I make sure she—it is usually a girl—has made a note of all the pauses and cuts. Actually, we very seldom make any cuts.

Before the cast leaves the theatre, the procedure at dress

rehearsal is carefully explained. Members of the cast are not allowed to bring friends into the dressing rooms without permission. They must not go and sit in the auditorium during the rehearsal. If they are not required on stage, then they must go down to the dressing room, and either chat quietly, read a book or play a quiet game. (It is a common sight to see some of the cast busy doing homework at rehearsal.) We put a table handy for such members. Of course no transistor sets are allowed in the theatre. All make-up must be removed before they leave the theatre. To keep an eye on these regulations we have one or two adult stewards on duty in the dressing room—when we can get them. No artist must at any time be seen by a member of the audience in costume and make-up, only on the stage or in the dressing room.

I was horrified recently when I attended a very fine performance by a well-known dramatic society, and after the show was over, the cast stood in the corridors, just as they had come off stage, chatting with their friends.

This kind of behaviour brings down the image of a society quicker than anything. Actually it is a very good idea to arrange a spare room as a Green Room where actors and the public can meet after a performance to chat and discuss the show. If you can persuade your social committee to brew up all the better. You might be able to enrol a few new members and make additional funds at the same time.

There are all kinds of special arrangements which have to be made for the dress rehearsal and the rest of the week. We have a decent kitchen backstage and arrange that tea, sugar and milk are available so that those members of the cast who come straight from work to the theatre can brew tea and cook a snack if they wish. The girls draw up a rota, so that at least a drink is ready every evening.

Our Social Committee always arranges for tea and biscuits to be served to the cast, stage staff and anyone who is involved in the production on dress rehearsal evenings. We have two dress rehearsals, Monday and Tuesday evenings.

Sometimes certain members of the cast might have to be picked up from work and brought to the theatre.

I absolutely abhor a dress rehearsal where everyone is exhausted as they drift off home in the early hours of the morning.

For everyone, amateur or professional, a dress rehearsal is a severely taxing occasion. Because of the tension, nerves become frayed and tempers short. We try to overlook any display of rudeness. We just say to ourselves, 'Ah, dress rehearsal,' and let it go at that. Actually we have built up such a tradition over the years that it is seldom we experience any serious lapse from the normal. Actual temperament we would never tolerate. I do not think we have had more than a couple of such displays since the Theatre was founded. Of course, we are all human, and at times we have to be very careful. Tact and a smile can demolish most edifices built of outraged vanity.

Because many of our members are young, I try to avoid late rehearsals. My views on this point are expressed elsewhere in this book. Of recent years we have managed things fairly well in this respect. Our latest time has been half past nine.

This does mean that we seldom complete a full rehearsal of the play in the evening. Whilst this is not ideal, I still maintain it is better, because we have time to re-work a sound effect, rephrase a weak ending of a scene, or a scene change or do any of the little things which need extra attention and which make the show that little nearer perfection. Having two nights we can do this and still finish at a reasonable time.

Every night of the week during the run of a show, I go straight from school to the theatre, usually arriving at about half past four. Members of the cast are asked to be at the theatre no later than 6 o'clock, particularly if there is a large cast.

The make-up team arranges a detailed list of the cast in the exact order in which they are to be made up. I do my best to persuade them to learn how to make themselves up although character make-up, in the case of young people, requires a second person to help.

There is no need for the market-place chaos so often found in dressing rooms. Quiet insistence on a plan of behaviour means a quiet, orderly way of preparation. I am available to anyone who wishes to consult me. The Stage Manager and his staff are busy on the stage. Make-up, Wardrobe and Social Committee personnel are all intently occupied with their various duties, and the cast, hiding the butterflies by strenuous exertion in the business of getting ready, are all dressing.

The dress rehearsal is scheduled to start at 7 o'clock. Sometimes, because of matters outside our control (such as a United match which nearly always disrupts traffic schedules) we are a little later. Seldom are we later than 7.30.

No strangers are allowed in the theatre to watch rehearsals unless permission has been granted specifically. I am quite prepared to allow any interested person or group to watch if they would like, provided they make the request to me.

On one occasion there was an unpleasant scene when three complete strangers parked themselves at the back of the theatre, and when asked what they were doing there, most rudely asserted that they had come to watch the rehearsal. I had never seen them in my life before, and asked them politely to remove themselves. They then became disgustingly abusive. Only when I said I would have no alternative but to send for the police did they go. This sort of thing is typical of the gross bad manners which surround us today.

I prefer to sit in the darkened auditorium and watch, only stopping the rehearsal when I must. I like to run through the scene, my notebook on my knee, sitting in different parts of the theatre to test sightlines and audibility.

I sometimes plant several people about the auditorium to test the audibility of the cast, particularly when there are several new members in the cast.

At the end of that scene, the characters are called on to the stage and I go through the notes I have taken. If things are going reasonably well and there are no scene changes, I like to do this at the end of the full act.

Any very weak move or piece of dialogue is run through again. Particular attention is paid to openings and endings of scenes. Speed is attended to and perhaps a sound effect retimed or a lighting change rehearsed or altered. I dislike making any alterations at this stage, but sometimes it has to be done.

Any sign of undue excitement at these rehearsals is quickly controlled. It would be fatal to let it grow. Do that and the result can be near hysteria. A reasoned, firm but kind approach is all that is required.

On the notice board in the main dressing room is put a complete cast list. As each member of the cast arrives he puts a tick by his name. I keep an eye on this list myself.

We have a call boy who, under orders from the Stage Manager, goes down to the dressing room at the half-hour, quarter-hour, ten minutes, five minutes, and then about two minutes before Curtain Up he shouts, 'Beginners please'. That is the signal for all the cast appearing in the first act to take their places either on stage or in the wings in readiness for their entrances.

On the Tuesday night dress rehearsal we finish off the play and discuss any adjustments necessary. I give the cast an opportunity to ask questions, and then we very carefully rehearse the curtain call. I consider a bad curtain call is fatal. It creates a shoddy impression for the audience to take home.

Another point which is carefully arranged: the press usually contact me a day or two before our dress rehearsal and we agree at what time they will come to take photographs. I cannot speak too highly of the courtesy and co-operation I have received at the hands of the press. Reporters and photographers have always been helpful and understanding. They have never caused any unnecessary interruption and have come at the times I have named. Such consideration when the air is electric with tension is kindness indeed.

Before I send everyone home at the end of the rehearsal, I gather them all together and give them a word of thanks for their effort. Just the most important 'musts' are briefly mentioned. There is nothing left now but prayer.

On the opening night I chat to anybody and everybody, wish them the best of luck and then slip up on the stage. There I have a last reassuring word with the Stage Manager and his staff, and make a few short announcements over the microphone. I pay our respects to any V.I.P.'s out front, give out the notices about interval refreshments, the raffle and further performances. I then slip out to my seat at the back of the auditorium with my notebook. From this point, the show is in the hands of the Stage Manager.

After I have left the stage, the Stage Manager takes the last glance around the stage. If he is satisfied that all is in order, he gives the signal, 'Tabs Away', the 'Electrics' presses a button. With a soft whirr, the curtains slide apart. Another show is on the way.

This next season I think we shall dispense with front tabs, and try the open stage technique. It can be effective, but it can also be a failure. To be fully successful, I think there needs to be an apron stage.

The Front of House staff is in charge of our Business Manager, Miss Blodwyn Williams. She briefs her programme sellers, and Miss Best who is C.O. in charge of raffles. Refreshments are served in a room just off the foyer. Tea, minerals and biscuits are sold. Sometimes, if we have a heavy booking of children, we sell ice-cream. Chocolates and sweets are on sale on the landing just outside the doors of the auditorium.

Usually in the first interval, if there is more than one, the representatives of the press come into the dressing room to ask any questions about the cast or the play and to take a cup of tea with us. They can then chat to the cast if they so wish, and this, I have always felt, is one of the things which makes for a happy relationship between the theatre and the press.

Just about the most amusing anecdote of our history took

place at the interval of the first Shakespeare we ever did. We were presenting *A Midsummer Night's Dream*. A cub reporter, complete with notebook and pencil, was asking me questions. He had covered the cast and points of the production. As the warning bell he said, 'Oh, there's just one question I'd like to ask. Is this the first time this play has been done?'

I gasped. Then I could not resist it. With a poker face I said, 'Yes. The author is in the audience.'

At the end of the performance, we sometimes have visitors backstage. The Mayor of the borough is usually our Patron. We have a visit from quite a few civic dignitaries in the course of a season. Our chairman, a very busy man, seldom misses the last night of a production.

Sometimes we invite children and their teachers from visiting schools to meet the cast after a show.

After a performance of *Heidi*, we had a visit from a party of children from the Royal Schools for the Deaf, in Old Trafford. They showed great delight at meeting the cast. One of their number thanked the company for a very enjoyable evening.

After the opening performance, I briefly run through my notes taken during the evening. I deal with general faults first, and then with individual mistakes. These latter I quietly discuss with the individual concerned. This method causes less embarrassment.

On the evening of the second performance we usually have one press report to hand. Whilst not putting too much importance on the printed criticism, it is only natural that the youngsters are keen to see what someone outside the Theatre thinks about the show.

It is interesting to note that there is very little evidence of jealousy. If there is any it is kept severely in check. Any adverse criticism is discussed at length, and if it is just, due attention paid to it.

After the final performance, I call stage staff, cast, Wardrobe, Make-up group, Front of House staff and the Social

Committee and tender them my thanks. Many a tired conscientious helper is made happy by a simple 'Thank you'. The brash know-alls we encounter so frequently today look upon such courtesy as weakness. I prefer to be such a weakling.

The stage staff has a heavy task when the final curtain falls. They have to dismantle the set and take it down to the cellar. This is very hard going, as is all their work. I heartily wish we could get more help, particularly in this department of the Theatre. I would like sufficient people to arrange two or three teams. Then perhaps a team could do just one show per season. This would make much less harassing for the stage manager.

I cannot speak too highly of the work done by the stage staff. Constantly am I reminded that this Theatre is a team effort. Without this concept, it would collapse.

As I leave the theatre to catch my train home, with yet another show behind me, tired but happy, my brain is a whirling mass of ideas concerned—with our next show. The last thing I did before I left the theatre was to announce to the cast the auditions for our next production—the next Wednesday night.

22

Social Activities

We are a theatre, and our first aim is to present plays of all kinds and involve our members in some way in our productions. The Headquarters is the centre where we meet, rehearse, make costumes and properties and discuss all the aspects of theatre which interest us.

Unless we are doing a show with a large cast, many of our members are not actively involved. It is essential that the interest of these youngsters should be kept alive in some way. Here again, if we had more helpers, we could do so much more. We arrange a varied series of activities which keep us all busy. Our season lasts all the year round. The Headquarters is only officially closed one week per year. Even then I am in the house some of the time.

We have frequent meetings of our various committees. On these occasions a social atmosphere develops. Free discussion takes place, refreshments are served and new members are quickly absorbed into the main stream of the Theatre.

'Open' evenings are popular. Members are encouraged to bring a friend. They can give turns. In this relaxed atmosphere I am able to pick out potential performers. The hut at the rear of the premises is regularly the scene of the weird shaking which today passes for dancing. Usually one of our groups provides the rhythm.

From time to time visiting lecturers come along to give us the value of their experiences on many topics. I borrow a projector if they bring films or slides. Most of the topics deal with some aspect of theatre though other subjects are not taboo.

A few years ago we were visited by a concert party artist who was 'resting' in Manchester. He had seen our notice board outside and, intrigued, called in for information. He became a constant visitor. Cultured, clever, with a genial nature, he gave us three evenings' entertainment in the form of character studies from Dickens and the Classics as a thank-offering for the pleasant times he had spent with us. We were thrilled.

Quite my 'squareness' amuses my youngsters. Since they know I am open to conviction, much energy is mustered to convert me. After a particularly long serious argument one evening, I made them an offer. If they would listen to some classical music, then I would do my best to endure a beat session. They could explain why they were 'sent' by this cacophony of sound.

They accepted my gesture and two boys prepared for the opening session. I was much impressed when I saw with what seriousness they set about their task. They borrowed books from the library. From these they illustrated their points. Selections from relevant records were played. It was a stimulating and interesting evening and I can truthfully say that since that lecture I have accepted the beat world with more interest and a less jaundiced ear. I regret that we did not get a complete record of that evening on tape. The two lecturers are now in a well-known rhythm group which has figured in the Top Twenty.

The classical evening was also a success. They listened to a symphony and part of a piano concerto. Searching questions were asked and answered to our mutual satisfaction.

We take photographs of our productions. When I lecture about the theatre I take these slides along. Occasionally we have an evening when we run a selection of the slides through for members and friends. This helps in a recruiting capacity.

After our producton of *Richard III* we threw the Head-quarters open to the public one evening. We had costumes, props, scenery and designs on view. Members of the cast, in costume, took visitors round, explaining our activities and answering questions. In one room our lighting expert was showing slides of the show. Our Registrar was enrolling new members and interviewing prospective patrons. The coffee bar was open and did good business.

We extend a hearty welcome to interested individuals or groups to spend an evening with us. Dramatic societies, students from training colleges and youth clubs visit us. Visitors are invited to ask questions. We like visitors to come to what we call Magazine Evening. About a dozen members choose a story, an extract from a book or a scene from a play. They are encouraged to read it to the assembled members. If they are shy, then another member reads the selection. If they wish, they can play a musical instrument or their favourite selection on the record player. We have had original compositions offered to us.

From time to time we have a rhythm group of our own. For several years we had a very fine one, the Top Five. Their playing was a pleasure for even a 'square' to listen to. They were also pleasant on the eye. Good-looking, with tidy hair styles and spotlessly clean, they dressed in white shirts, scarlet bows, tight black trousers, and scarlet cummerbunds. They broke up when two turned professional. A third has now got his commission in the RAF.

As I know John English personally, and am so thrilled about his Midlands Arts Centre for Youth, I was anxious for our members to see this wonderful centre. We arranged to visit this materialization of a dream, and had a most inspiring day. We are now arranging another party. It is in such places as this that I see coming alive all the ideals I have dreamt about for forty years. The zest of youth for these things is there. It is our bounden duty to give youth the opportunity. The reward for the lover of the arts is an intoxication—the sheer delight in being alive, and responding to all the beauty around us.

On odd occasions over the years we have had a poetry reading session among ourselves. We have had friends in to join with us and I intend to plan a more ambitious pro-

The author in action during rehearsal

Preparatory talks for *Richard III*

Spring-cleaning
the headquarters

The sound effects
man

gramme. I hope to arrange a group of about twenty who will get together and work out some themes. We shall then find poems to fit the themes, together with pieces of music, and guitarists. I suggest that the readers will be on stage, picked out by spotlights. I would like to see a programme presented about once a month.

We sometimes have a folk group in the cellars. It is our boast that we never close. During the summer we try out new ideas. Thank goodness we always have plenty of those!

M

23

Marionettes

Ever since I saw a Punch and Judy Show when I was about three years of age, puppets and marionettes have fascinated me. After reading about this absorbing art form, I long intended starting a group.

When the famous Walter Wilkinson brought his puppets to Manchester I was an enthralled spectator. I had met Waldo and Muriel Lanchester and watched their amazing marionettes, and had taken some boys from school to see the Hogarth Puppets. Just before we founded the Theatre, I had started a group in my school.

We built our marionettes from Waldo Lanchester's designs and constructed a portable theatre. So well were our little people received that we set out to prepare a full-length show.

Every boy in this group joined the Children's Theatre. We set out to make some money for the Theatre and were prepared to give a show anywhere for expenses and a donation. Very soon we were in great demand. We appeared at children's parties, church bazaars, works' parties and even at weddings. In about four years we travelled over three thousand miles, and netted a healthy sum for the Theatre. In doing this we had a fascinating time.

One by one the boys in the group left school, started keeping company steadily with their girl friends or were sent to work away from Manchester. The actual puppets, which had become our friends, grew battered. They lost limbs, cracked and disintegrated. The marionette group faded away.

Only last week, in a box in school I found a discoloured little figure. It was the forlorn little clown. It was Chico, the first figure I had ever made. Rather sadly I picked it out of the box. I remember the boy who used to manipulate Chico. He is now the father of a family. I felt a strong urge to form another group. I glanced at my rehearsal time-table for my next show. Alas, if only I could keep going on two hours' sleep each night.

I strongly recommend the formation of a marionette group. It is an exciting and rewarding project. It is a hobby which stimulates the imagination, and, once begun, becomes absorbing.

Should you go to Stratford-upon-Avon, pay a visit to Mr Waldo Lanchester's shop in Henley Street, almost opposite Shakespeare's birthplace. Mr Lanchester is a genial and helpful person. He will answer your queries, and give you all the information to start you off on the enchanting trail into the magic land of puppetry.

I always feel when I hold a puppet and await the rise of the curtain, a little as God may have felt as he looked at the first man at the beginning of the world.

24

Ex-Members

At no time have we ever looked upon our Theatre as a training ground for the professional stage.

To implant a love and appreciation of the live theatre and to enrich the lives of our members, encouraging them to take an active attitude to life, rather than a passive one, is the sum total of our aims.

Nevertheless, arising from the fact that hundreds of youngsters have since April, 1945, been introduced to the magic of the theatre, it is understandable that some of them have developed the urge to tread the boards. Some have succeeded in getting there and have made a name for themselves.

Our most famous 'old girl' is of course June Ritchie. June joined the Theatre when she was nine years old. From the very first evening, when she came to watch a rehearsal, she won our hearts. Her round, bonny face, out of which shone a pair of sparkling eyes which mirrored all the excitement she felt, was alive. She had then, and still has a rich, warm personality. When she told me that she had set her heart on going to RADA, and was then successful in getting a scholarship, I personally had qualms. I would never allow myself to do anything to shatter anyone's dreams, particularly those of a young person, but I have always felt that some of the larger drama schools tend to crush a student's personality. June had such a rich personality that it would have been a tragedy had her training turned her into a puppet. Thank God it did not do that.

I remember an evening spent with June in the Midland

Hotel in Manchester when she was filming *A Kind of Loving*. I repeated my appeal that she should retain her naturalness. She smiled at my earnestness, and I felt as I talked with her that nothing would ever take away or change the fundamental June. I met her when she was playing in *Too True to be Good* and we had tea together. The same ebullient, straightforward personality looked out at me over the tea cup. She was still full of the earnest desire to do better. She was still June.

I am sorry to see so little of her. To know I was able to help June in her early days, and guide her steps if only on the first rung of the ladder of her career, will ever give me deep satisfaction and pride.

Whatever part June played for me, she put every bit of herself into her performance. In 1952 we put on *Twelfth Night*. At the first performance, at the interval, I was approached by the critic of the *Manchester Evening News*. He frankly admitted that he had not expected our standard to be so high. He asked me to sit with him during the second half of the show. As he watched, he became quite excited, picking out various things which particularly appealed to him. Suddenly he gripped my arm, and hoarsely whispered, 'Look at that little girl. She has not a word to say, but she is acting with every fibre of her body.' That little girl was June.

From time to time she had expressed the view that she would like to go on the stage. I have always been chary of encouraging youngsters to go on the boards, knowing how difficult it is to make a success of it. Yet, if they really make up their minds to take up a stage career, then I will do all I can to help, providing they have talent. June was offered a scholarship to RADA and was given a county grant.

During her sojourn at RADA she won various awards for excellence of work, including special training for singing. She had always had a pleasant singing voice. At the end of each year, Emile Littler presents two prizes of twenty-five guineas to the two students who are the most promising. When June left, the two prizes were amalgamated, and she was awarded fifty guineas.

Her meteoric flash to fame in her first film, *A Kind of Loving* with Alan Bates and Thora Hird, needs no elaboration from me.

Another well-known personality who for a short time was a member of our Theatre, is the TV newscaster Brian Trueman. In our first Shakespearean production *A Midsummer Night's Dream*, Brian played Lysander. His performance was hailed by the press as outstanding. A most talented, open-hearted young man, he was one of the most popular members we have ever had. We have all watched his career with the greatest interest.

The first time we played *The Merchant of Venice* was in 1951. The Prince of Aragon was played by John Ross who gave a notable performance. When John left school, he went into rep. He played on both sound radio and television. Then after several years he gave up the stage and now is with a business house in Manchester.

In our musicals some years ago, we had an outstanding and handsome lead. Stuart Simpson was a gifted artist when he was very young. He had appeared on the stage as a tap dancer and entertainer for several years before he joined the Theatre. When he was sixteen he went into revue and toured for several years. One of his engagements was in one of Tessie O'Shea's shows at the London Palladium. Eventually he left the stage. He came back to us and played in a few shows with great distinction. He is now in the Manchester business world.

In 1958 we produced *Hamlet*. Our Ophelia, Marjorie Westgate, and her fiancé Joseph Seed as Hamlet gave performances that are talked of today. I recall that, not long before our production, Marjorie complained that I had not paid enough attention to her in rehearsal. She said that she felt completely bewildered. I explained that I had deliberately arranged it that way. That was how I wished it to be played.

I have always felt that the interpretation of Ophelia's part as a demented girl chasing round like a startled mare at an agricultural show means that the stark horror of her madness is dissipated, leaving a feeling of jagged incompleteness. Marjorie realized what I was aiming at. She played her part with gentle bewildered gestures, her facial expressions conveying that terrifying vacuity of madness, where there is a complete loss of touch with the world of reality. Her meeting with Laertes was staggeringly poignant. Marjorie became a student at the Library Theatre in Manchester, married our Hamlet, and family ties won.

The girl with the flowing hair who played Lewis Carroll's Alice for me was Cynthia Sallabank. She took many parts with distinction, scoring a real hit in *The Lady's Not for Burning*. She studied Dress Design at art school, but the lure of the boards was too strong. Television appearances and a short period at Oldham Rep. have been followed by an engagement at the Library Theatre, Manchester where, she is appearing as I write.

David Duffy, well known on the TV screen, is another ex-member of the Theatre. Two other members of the cast of our *The Lady is not for Burning* are now professionals, Chris Fox and Brian Davies. Several others have gone to various drama schools, and entered the entertainment world. Some I have lost track of, others contact me spasmodically. I recently heard of one well on the way to becoming a television producer. This is the second who has succeeded in this field to my knowledge.

In different parts of England there are some of our ex-members who are teachers of drama. It is thrilling to know that the torch we lighted in our Headquarters is being carried throughout the land.

When these offspring of the Theatre call to see me, their starry-eyed enthusiasm is a wonderful antidote to the apathetic poison we have had to combat over the years.

25

Our Record

As previously stated, we did not get down to staging a production in our first year. Our time was spent in meetings where we discussed ways and means of making a start on actual production. I seemed to spend all my time trying to convince people, who did not wish to be convinced, that our Theatre was a practical possibility. I had to explain away the myriad difficulties which our opponents, and even members of the Committee, brought up with regular and persistent confidence. I often left our meetings physically and mentally exhausted after having implored someone to allow us to try something, rather than consign the idea to Hades before it saw the light of day. Such efforts tend to leave one depressed, and with no energy to continue the fight. As I sipped a cup of tea on reaching home, I began to have qualms with increasing regularity.

I had been suffering for months from sciatic pains. Being so full of plans, I had not bothered to visit my doctor. Well-wishing friends had swamped me with cures, each assuring me that their particular one was the sovereign remedy. But, in spite of aspirin, codeine, and a host of soothing agents, I gradually got worse. For nine weeks I lay flat on my back, unable to move. Then, after an operation I was a further eight weeks learning to walk again. On returning to school I had to take things quietly for another six weeks, so we had to curtail Committee meetings, though we did manage to keep the pot boiling.

In 1945 I was introduced to some members of the Manchester section of the Free Austrian Movement in Great

Britain. In the autumn of this year we did a joint show with them in the Moselsy Street Adult Education Centre. We shared the profits. Our share was just under four pounds. This was a start, but I did not consider this as a Children's Theatre production.

Our first show was a revue, *The Coffee Stall*, on which I have already commented. We were gratified with the result and saw great possibilities for the future. I felt the show had made a ripple on the surface of local life, and perhaps good would develop from it.

In the November we put on a junior revue, *Dots and Dashes*. The emphasis in this show was on the younger members. There was a fine mime arranged by the headmistress of a junior school. This co-operation made me feel that perhaps the prejudice against us was cracking.

A particularly novel spot in this show was a most professional conjuring turn by a twelve-year-old boy, and we discovered a thirteen-year-old girl who had an outstanding voice. Press notices were good and the general opinion was that we should present a pantomime.

I thought this was a good idea, and accordingly we presented *Cinderella*. We were still in the throes of austerity living. I wrote the book of the show myself. The Baron became Baron Black Market, the Ugly Sisters were Plastic and Nylon, and the Broker's Men were two spivs, Fiddler and Drone. It turned out to be a slick moving show with an outstanding Buttons in the person of Jimmy Donigan. Our image advanced a little in the eyes of the Stretfordians who realized we were aiming to achieve a higher standard than usually found in local societies.

I did not feel I had sufficient material to do something of a more valuable content, so we decided in April 1948 to do another revue-type entertainment.

We planned to do two nights and hired a hall in the centre of Stretford. Mainly due I think to bad publicity, we sold practically no tickets. And to make things worse, the night we opened was the night Manchester United football team brought home the cup they had won the previous Saturday at Wembley. You can well imagine where the people of Stretford where that night.

We played to about thirty people. As we had sold only three tickets for the next night, we had a hurried meeting, decided to cut our losses and cancelled the performance scheduled for the next night. This was nearly the death knell of the Stretford Children's Theatre.

Under the direction of their headmaster, Mr J. Thompson, the Seymour Park Junior School had given a charming little musical, *A Royal Jester*, in their school hall. In furtherance of my desire that all schools should participate in our Theatre, I asked Mr Thompson if he would put this show on for us. He agreed, and it was staged in the Lostock school on 5th May, 1948. It was a memorable performance, but the audience was small.

Following on our heavy losses the general outspoken opinion was that we should drop the whole idea. But my Lincolnshire blood was up. Nothing would have induced me to have given in. I was determined to carry on if I had to do it alone.

In the November we put on three one-act plays. They were: *All the Tea in China* by Wilfred Harvey, *Safe Custody* by F. Austin Hyde and *The Cardinal's Revenge* by B. H. Holland. The last I had written for the boys in my school, in particular for one boy, Joseph Seed. He had joined the Theatre saying he did not want to act but I was confident he would make a good actor. For a few months I played him on the line. He helped backstage. Then he walked on. In my play he took the part of Emilio, the old silversmith who provides the villain with the poisoned casket. Joe played Oberon in our first Shakespeare, then Shylock, a most memorable performance. He continued to give marvellous performances in varied parts including the Mikado, and finishing with a mammoth Hamlet. He was one of the finest artists we ever had.

In February, 1948, we staged *Dick Whittington and his Cat*.

I wrote the book, and with a cast of fifty, we put over a jolly, romping show. The audiences were a little larger which gave us more heart.

For some time the Stretford Corporation had been busy turning their Public Hall into a Civic Theatre. With many unavoidable inadequacies, they had succeeded in providing a centre where plays could be presented on a stage.

It was to be officially opened on Saturday, 26th March, 1949, to the public, and we were invited to present our *Dick Whittington*.

In the presence of our Mayor and Councillors we displayed our paces. I chafed inwardly, as I had my mind on a show of a more worth-while content. Nevertheless I was proud of my youngsters who were honourably mentioned in the leader of the local paper the following week.

From then on our productions were as follows:

1949   September 30th–October 1st
Ace, King, Queen A Revue.

I had a great idea when I planned this show: I visualized the cast dressed as a complete pack of cards. We were to play a game of whist to music. Basically a married couple invite two friends in for a game of cards. Two boy scouts come in to baby-sit and incidentally supplied the humour. But the best plans go awry. Attendances at rehearsal were never good. We had not got into our stride. The show turned out to be a modified game. It was fair, but I felt frustrated.

1949   November 18th, 19th
Three one-act Plays
Send Her Victorious by Philip Johnson
The Distant Drum by Philip Johnson
Beauty Is Fled by Paul Vincent Carroll

The first was produced by two teachers. They assured me, they had never realized it meant such hard work!

I produced the second, and the third, a delightful play was produced very well by Miss Mabel Bagley.

1949   December 15th–17th
Rumpelstiltskin by Bertram H. Holland

This was a great improvement. Excellent comedy was supplied by a perfect team, James Donigan and Malcolm Carter. We were at last reaching something we could call a standard.

1950   March 9th–11th
A Midsummer Night's Dream by William Shakespeare

'*A Midsummer Night's Dream* has proved what its producer has always believed—that children can and do enjoy Shakespeare when it is presented to them properly.'

Manchester Evening News

1950   November 9th–12th
Three One-act Plays
The Doubtful Misfortunes of Li Sing by Neil Tuson
Beauty is Fled by Paul Vincent Carroll
In Waltz Time by Philip Johnson.

These plays were well received. Each had a charm of its own. The second was repeated by request.

1951   January 19th–22nd
The Land of the Christmas Stocking
by Henry D. G. Foord and Mabel Buchanan

I have already mentioned the merits of this show. It was our greatest success to date.

1951   March 29th–31st April 2nd
The Merchant of Venice by William Shakespeare

This was a triumph. At last I was getting somewhere. 'Action and diction were generally on a high level, and costumes and scenery, made and painted by themselves, were as fresh as paint.

'Joseph Seed's Shylock was the work of a born actor.'

Manchester Evening News

1951   May 2nd–5th
Little Women Adapted by Marion de Forest
from the book by Louisa M. Alcott

We had made a mistake in booking the Civic Theatre.
We had just a month to prepare this play. I consider this was
one of the most polished shows we have ever done. Sentimental story? Yes, but very human. We enjoyed doing it, the
audience loved it and our stock soared.

1951   November 15th–17th
Rouge et Noir Arranged by Bertram H. Holland

This colourful show set in the restaurant, the Rouge et Noir,
had décor and costumes in red and black. The outstanding
feature was some exceptionally good singing.

1952   March 22nd–26th
Twelfth Night by William Shakespeare

A very good production, much upset the 'knockers'.

On the Sunday, I received a phone call to say Countess
Olivia was down with a temperature of over a hundred.
Frantic phone calls and a mad rush by taxi, followed by a solo
rehearsal till midnight, resulted in the excellent performance
by the substitute. She had a script in her hand but had little
need to refer to it.

Part of the dress rehearsal was recorded by the BBC, and
went out on the air in Children's Hour.

1952   May 22nd–26th
She Stoops to Conquer by Oliver Goldsmith

A rip-roaring show with graceful charm portrayed by the
girls, and an outstanding Tony Lumpkin by Alan Frost.
Costumes were beautiful. I can recall Hilda's smile of happiness as I congratulated her.

1952   October 29th–November 1st
The Mikado by W. S. Gilbert and A. Sullivan

I have covered this show in the chapter on musicals.
Manchester Evening Chronicle said:

'They possess two vital factors in amateur productions, team spirit and co-operation.

'Pretty dark-haired Marjorie Vickers—and 189 other Stretford under 18-year-olds—are not much impressed by the statement that they are taking part in one of the most remarkable theatrical and sociological experiments in Britain today.

'As far as they are concerned, being members of Stretford Children's Theatre is just one of the nicest ways of spending their spare time.'

1953   January 30th–February 2nd
Where the Rainbow Ends by Clifford Mills and John Ramsay
This has adventure, melodrama and make-believe. Our members like the play, and made the audience like it too.

1953   March 25th–28th
Julius Caesar by William Shakespeare
We thoroughly enjoyed this exciting play. A special feature of this production was a flight of steps leading from the auditorium to the stage, enabling the crowd to surge up on to the stage. This added excitement to the action.

1953   May 13th–16th
The Scarlet Pimpernel by Baroness Orczy
This was a really memorable production. One of the papers pointed out that there was no need for critical indulgence as the acting could stand up to the most searching scrutiny.

We had a novel feature. I controlled the whole production from the back of the theatre with a walkie-talkie. A special point noted by everyone was the smooth running of the whole show. We were very gratified with the result.

1953   October 27th–30th
Daddy Long Legs by Jean Webster
A most enjoyable show. The outstanding point of this production was the delicate playing of the love scenes. Our standard improved with every show we put on.

1954   March 17th–20th
The Taming of the Shrew by William Shakespeare
'On many occasions Shakespeare must turn in his grave when amateurs "murder" his plays. But surely it is equally possible for Shakespeare to lie back with a smile of contentment, as he must have done this week, when Stretford Children's Theatre presented *The Taming of the Shrew*.'

Stretford and Urmston News.

I certainly smiled with pleasure at the applause that greeted the curtain calls in this show. I was deeply grateful for the effort my youngsters had put into their rehearsals.

1954   May 5th–8th
The Gondoliers by W. S. Gilbert and Arthur Sullivan
How we enjoyed preparing this gem! It certainly showed in the rapt attention and acclaim of the audiences. Our dancing has always been our weakest point, but not in this show. I have seldom seen such disappointed faces as there were in the dressing room on the night we finished the run. We would have liked to have played it for a month.

1954   Autumn
1066 and All That by Reginald Arkell and Alfred Reynolds.
This show was great fun, and a great test for the costume department who rose magnificently to the occasion. Since it had a large cast, it was a great opportunity to use members who had never been on the stage before. I was able to spot several potential leads for future show. This is much more satisfactory than the usual audition.

1955   January
Beauty and the Beast by Nicholas Stuart Gray
This is a most satisfying play to present. We had much larger audiences and felt that we had really consolidated our position as a sound group. For the first time I felt warmly satisfied, but not smugly so. We had to keep our standard. This meant hard work.

1955   March 16th–19th
Romeo and Juliet by William Shakespeare

This was our most ambitious show to date. I had looked forward to producing it as I was certain with June Ritchie we had the perfect Juliet. I was not mistaken. Two things remain in my mind—the fine speaking of the Shakespearean lines that we achieved, and Philip Doyle's fine sets. Our principals were good, but some of the smaller parts were a little weak. This is to be expected, although we do manage a fairly even standard these days.

The final scene, as the bereaved parents left the tomb and the footsteps of the guards faded away, when the lights dimmed and nothing was visible save the faint sheen of Juliet's dress, was a striking picture. Walford Davis's Solemn Melody surged out as the tabs closed, and the audience carried away a scene which would remain with them for a long time.

1955   May 12th–15th
Trial by Jury and *HMS Pinafore*
by W. S. Gilbert and Arthur Sullivan

Again we revelled in the colourful dialogue and delightful music. The male chorus was a bit weak, but our principals were excellent. We just happened to be lucky. I wish I had such a group of singers in the Theatre at the present time.

1955   October 12th–15th
The Quaker Girl by Lionel Monckton

We decided to do another musical whilst we had our singers. This was a most happy show. The youthful enthusiasm of our members burst through the production like the bubbles in the wedding-scene champagne. The rendering of the song 'Barbizon' stopped the show. A fine effort to remember.

1956   January 11th–14th
Alice in Wonderland by Lewis Carroll

I picked Cynthia Sallabank at the audition because she had long hair and look just like Alice. It was a gamble—I had

Romeo and Juliet, 1954, with June Ritchie
as Juliet

The two villains from *The Imperial
Nightingale*

Scene from *The Tinder Box*

Rehearsing *The Lady's not for Burning*

no idea whether she could act. My hunch came off. The costumes were most attractive. A most unique feature was that we used the back projection method for our sets. The slides were brilliantly executed again by Philip Doyle. Although everyone seemed delighted, I felt the show dated, and frankly I felt the final result, though ably acted, was not really worth the time we had spent on it.

1956 March 7th–10th
School for Scandal by Richard Brinsley Sheridan

This show was not appreciated by the audience. I was pleased with the quality of the acting. The scenes with Sir Peter and Lady Teazle were most delicately done, and the comedy well brought out, yet it seemed to fall on deaf ears. We were disappointed, as the whole cast and backstage staff had spared no effort. This can so easily happen when a company offers quality. It makes it rather disheartening.

1956 May 9th–12th
Ten Little Niggers by Agatha Christie

This was our first thriller. It was thoroughly enjoyed both by cast and audiences. The outstanding performance was given by Joseph Seed as the Judge. Another fine study was that of General Mackenzie, played by David Shawcross.

1956 October 17th–20th
Patience by W. S. Gilbert and Arthur Sullivan

This was one of our most effective productions. Gaiety and zest were its keynotes. We had a group of superb principals, and most people felt that it was sheer delight from beginning to end.

The Stretford and Urmston News said: 'Much insincere praise has been showered upon amateur shows, a fact which serves only to make it harder for a critic to describe achievement when he meets it. But here at Stretford is a wealth of singing and acting talent sufficient to stagger those who discover it for the first time.'

N

1957   January 16th–19th
The Marvellous Story of Puss in Boots by Nicholas Stuart Gray
This was the least successful of the Gray plays we have done.
Several contributory causes were responsible. Many in-
terruptions occurred during rehearsals which made a
difference. The audiences seemed to enjoy the show, but it
lacked polish, and I was far from satisfied.

1957   May 1st–4th
The Arcadians by Lionel Monckton
In spite of the doubts of this choice by followers of our work,
this was another triumph for the whole company. Pat
Stokes in the part of Sombra gave a magnificent performance.
Although the show had an adult flavour, our cast revelled in
the fun.

1957   October 16th–19th
The Mikado by W. S. Gilbert and Arthur Sullivan
We had been urged for some time to repeat this show. The
popular opinion was that no allowance need be made because
of the youth of our cast. The press pointed out that Neville
Jackson's Pooh Bah and Joseph Seed's Mikado would have
graced the best adult company. Naturally we were tremen-
dously exhilarated.

1957   December 4th–7th
Cinderella by V. C. Clinton-Baddeley
This was a delightful show. We enjoyed the lovely tunes and
the rich humour. Buttons, played with sheer artistry by Roy
Jackson, lifted the show on to a higher plane than is usually
achieved in pantomime. This was due to Roy's talent and an
excellent script and music.

Roy won the 'Prompter's Palm' for the best comedy part
played in the Manchester area. This is a trophy offered for
outstanding performances in Amateur Drama.

1958   February 5th–8th
The Heartless Princess by Franklyn Black

This was an unusual play in which we revelled. The roguish Fox is a delightful part and we seemed to get every bit of humour out of him. Our standard in this show nearly satisfied me. It is an excellent play to do in a school. The construction is peculiar, but the characters and situations are attractive, and the cast enjoy doing it.

'*The Heartless Princess* is a dramatized fable to be acted by adults for children. But the Stretford Children's Theatre which tackles anything from Shakespeare to musical comedy, steps in and gets away with it.

'The acting of some of these children is so mature that in character parts where make-up and costumes provide opportunities for "disguise", it is well nigh impossible to assess their ages.'

Manchester Evening News

1958   May 12th–15th
Hamlet by William Shakespeare

I have commented on this production in my chapter on Shakespeare. It more than justified my claims that young people could understand and give good performances in a Shakespeare play. Many people came to scoff, but left the theatre very impressed. Each night members of the audience came to confess this frankly to me, and to admit they had changed their views about youth theatre. One very well-known producer in the North of England came to see the production three times, and confessed he was more impressed each time he saw it.

1958   October 29th–November 1st
The Imperial Nightingale by Nicholas Stuart Gray

This is a sheer delight to play. I felt our scenic department showed up well in this production. Our sets were simple and most effective. Costumes matched the sets, and the whole show had that satisfying all of quality. The joy I have had

from the effort of our members through the years is such that
I could never express it fully in words.

1959   January 21st–24th
Alice, Thomas and Jane

I had seen this play performed several years ago and had
always promised myself that we would do it. I found it was
out of print, but was lucky. The Altrincham Garrick Society,
whom I had seen doing the play, kindly lent me two copies.
This meant copying parts, but the youngsters so liked the
play that it was a labour of love.

Our Alice, an eight-year-old, captured the hearts of the
audiences from curtain rise to fall. The press called her 'a
pint-sized redhead with a melting smile'.

1959   April 22nd–25th
Love from Judy from the book by Jean Webster

'A magnificent performance of *Love From Judy* by Stretford
Children's Theatre last night at the Civic Theatre turned an
audience, which included scores of schoolchildren, into the
most attentive "house" I have seen.

'It is another triumph for producer Bert Holland, who is
doing such wonderful work with these children, and a
reflection on the public-mindedness of the Stretford people
that there should ever be an empty seat at these shows.

'The acting is superb.

'There is not a senior drama society anywhere that could
have cast it better, and the performance of 17-year-old
June Ritchie as Judy would have graced a professional
production.'

Manchester Evening Chronicle

1959   October 14th–17th
A Girl called Jo from the book by Louisa M. Alcott

We were the first amateur society to do this show. I enjoyed
preparing it. The story is that of *Little Women*. Somehow we
did not quite get it over and it was a near flop. Some of the

principals took their rehearsals a little too casually. They were insecure in their interpretation, and consequently to me the whole thing lacked our usual smoothness and ease. It was laboured and disappointed me. The audiences assured us they had enjoyed it. Personally I was glad to see the final curtain.

1960   January 20th–23rd
The Land of the Christmas Stocking
by Henry D. G. Foord and Mabel Buchanan

This was a repeat, and went down with a swing. One paper pointed out that the Theatre was the envy of other towns, and Stretford should be ashamed to allow an empty seat.

Twenty minutes before curtain up on the opening night, we got a message to say that the boy playing Wee Willie Winkie, a leading part, could not appear. I called for a volunteer to read in the part. One little girl, Joan Keeling, who had watched rehearsals thought she knew some of the lines. She took over the part, and never faltered. One of the Manchester papers said this could not have happened in an adult society. It certainly spoke well of our *esprit de corps*.

1960   May 18th–21st
The Green Planet by Frank Harris

The author of this piece is a local person and originally wrote it for the Altrincham Garrick Society. It is just the thing for a juvenile audience. The whole plot centres round a space ship and the adventures of its crew on the Green Planet. We had to enlist the help of one or two children who had never appeared on the stage before. This made the show a little uneven, but nevertheless it was an enjoyable production.

1960   October 12th–15th
Meet me by Moonlight by Anthony Lesser

This is a delightful musical, set in Victorian England. Two features make it a most suitable choice even for modest societies. There are only nine characters, and the songs can be successfully put over without requiring specially good singing voices. Furthermore only one set is needed. I never remember a show where rehearsals went so smoothly. The dress rehearsal was surprisingly good, and the whole week a success. We were all satisfied with this show. I contemplate giving it again.

1961   January 25th–28th
The Windmill Man by Frederick Bowyer

This was another repeat show. Although it 'dates' in many ways, it is nevertheless a happy play to do. The press was unanimous in its assessment of the standard of acting and production. Quoting the television advertisement they said, 'They are consistently good'.

One critic said, 'Having spent a fair part of my working hours watching—sometimes enduring—amateur theatricals, I can only say this to Mr Holland and his charming company, thanks for a fine show and for the banishment of cynicism as regards all such companies.'

1961   May 2nd–6th
The Housemaster by Ian Hay

'Refreshingly entertaining, this excellent production by Stretford's Children's Theatre would jolt some of the critics of modern teenagers. None of the cast is more than eighteen, but their poise and assurance would credit an adult amateur company.

'Sixteen-year-old Roy Jackson adds to his reputation as one of the best juvenile actors in Greater Manchester.'

Manchester Evening News

1961   October 11th–14th
The Lady's not for Burning by Christopher Fry

'A Children's Theatre that would put many professionals to shame will lose about £80 this week—because they have no audience.

'Last night—with only 45 others I saw a performance of

The Lady's not for Burning at the Stretford Children's Theatre. Empty seats numbered 30–1. Yet the enthusiasm of the with teenagers in the play would have carried any audience them.

'I felt humbled when I went backstage, and they asked their producer eagerly, "Are there any more in tonight, Mr Holland?"

'How can we expect the theatre to survive when we squeeze the very spirit out of it?

'The youngsters' grasp of Christopher Fry's imagery was superb.'

Margaret Roberts, *Daily Herald*

'The most we can do is regret that so many ignored a fruitful evening, and hope that next time they will not be so reluctant to visit this fine company, which must be Stretford's main theatrical asset.'

Stretford Journal

'In these days of careless speech, slang, and vocal gimmicks it is a pleasure to hear the English language spoken with purity. And at the Stretford Children's Theatre production of Christopher Fry's *The Lady's not For Burning* this pleasure is available to all.

'Sadly on the first night, the theatre was almost empty. How can a town the size of Stretford be so blind to the enterprise and talent on its own doorstep?

'The sheer poetry of Fry's classic is a joy, and the mastery with which these young players handled this ambitious production was astonishing when one realizes their extreme youth—the average age was sixteen.'

Sale Guardian

1962　January 24th–27th
Willow Pattern Dream by Bertram H. Holland
This was the first full-length play, apart from revues I wrote for our Theatre. The idea of this fantasy came to me lazing in a boat on the Avon at Stratford. I worked out much with

the youngsters during rehearsals. The general press view was that it was a delightful fantasy. I was gratified. It proved, I think, that we were versatile and had plenty of talent.

The Stretford Journal said: 'These children make regular pilgrimages to Manchester in search of good entertainment quite unnecessary for anyone with sense and sensibility.'

I am only too sorry that shortage of time prohibits me from attempting more original shows. It is interesting writing for these vital youngsters.

1962   May 23rd–26th
The Green Goddess by William Archer

'Has Stretford Children's Theatre produced yet another star of the future? This was the question intriguing the audience who saw Roy Jackson's brilliant performance in the leading role of the Raja, at the same theatre that fostered June Ritchie's early talent.

'Roy, who is eighteen, displayed maturity, grace and elegance, as well as the utmost confidence and an obvious gift for satirical imitation. He is certainly a boy to watch.

'All the cast looked as though they were enjoying every minute of this play—and that is what made it so successful. The cast was up to its usual very high standard.'

Manchester Evening News

1962   October 11th–13th
Tabs Away by Bertram H. Holland

My intention was for the members to prepare this entirely. It was planned in July that they should have everything in readiness for me to vet, prior to the final rehearsals. We arranged to meet in September but when we did I was bitterly disappointed. The ideas were there, some of them clever. The cast was mapped out, but little serious work had been done.

We set to work, and by dint of hard work, ran up a show in readiness for the scheduled dates. It was enjoyed, and some parts were excellent. On the whole I was disappointed. I felt it was not up to our usual standard. One good point emerged: we discovered some new talent.

1962   December 12th–15th
Beauty and the Beast by Nicholas Stuart Gray

We had frequently been asked to repeat this play. It proved as excellent a production as the first. I was particularly pleased with it because it displayed perfect team work. A twelve-year-old newcomer, Frank Swann, gave the character of 'Mikey' a most appealing quality, and his timing for laughter was phenomenal. The underlying symbolism was subtly brought out.

1962   December 19th
Carol Service and Nativity Play

For some years we had held a Carol Service in our head-quarters. This year we decided to launch out and have a choir to sing carols and also give a Nativity Play. I approached Miss V. Ashwell, Headmistress of the Girls' Grammar School, and asked her if she would allow her school choir to co-operate. This she generously agreed to do, and the result was some delightful singing.

Boys from the Old Trafford Secondary Boys' School gave a Nativity Play. At the last moment one of the cast fell ill so I decided to take the part myself. I had just come on the stage and said a few words, when everything went black. I managed to stagger to the side of the stage. Two of the staff caught me as I fell.

With great promptitude our 'Effects' man continued to read my part over the microphone, and the play was finished with aplomb. Just another example of the adaptability of youth in an emergency. The heat on the stage, plus the close-fitting hood and tight costume I was wearing, had caused me to faint. Some of our youngsters assured me it had made the show more exciting.

1963   February 20th–23rd
The Merchant of Venice by William Shakespeare

'Playgoers watching for the first time a performance by Stretford Children's Theatre cannot fail to be startled by the acting talent of the youngsters taking part.

'When so many amateur dramatic societies are content to produce drawing-room drama, Stretford Children's Theatre, which presented *The Merchant of Venice* last week, shines like a good deed in a naughty world.

'The production proved a delight to the attentive listener.

'Andrew portrayed Shylock with amazing skill.'

Manchester Evening News

1963   May 15th–18th
The Snow Queen by Suria Magito and Rudolf Weil

I think Hans Christian Andersen would have been delighted had he seen our production. Cast and audiences were in complete accord in this fairyland. The sets were authentic. I heard one young boy in the audience say he would like to go and play among the passages in the Ice Palace. We managed most realistic effects—all made from scraps thrown on the rubbish heap at a foam plastic factory—and had much fun in building the scenery.

1963   November 6th–9th
Julius Caesar by William Shakespeare

I was very gratified with this production. I have mentioned it in my chapter on Shakespeare. Our lighting was particularly effective. I was told by one experienced producer that our Theatre was the envy of amateur groups all over the country. I do not wish to be conceited, but this remark naturally brings a glow of satisfaction to the whole company.

1963   19th December
Nativity Play and Carol Service

By popular request we gave another Nativity Play in the Civic Theatre. Carols were sung by the choir of St Matthew's,

Stretford Parish Church. It was well attended. We would like this to be an annual event. It is rather difficult as so many school functions are held about this time. We shall, however, try to arrange it.

1964 January 30th–February 2nd
Rumpelstiltskin and the Three Wishes by Bertram H. Holland
This was my second full-length play specially written for the Theatre. It was a great occasion. I claim no great ability to write for young people, but I do know a little of what they like. In this show I gave them the lot and they lapped it up.

I quote the *Stretford Journal*, 'No producer of a professional pantomime could ever hope to hold his juvenile audience on such a taut string as did Mr Holland in this production. It showed imagination and sympathy for the children who made up his audiences. His use of music and a wide range of techniques showed a breadth of theatrical vision rare on the professional stage. The production sparkled throughout.

'Pulling the children through a maze of spells and black magic was Andrew Winton as the evil dwarf magician, Rumpelstiltskin, who combined wild and wide variations in his voice, extravagant and melodramatic movements of his small athletic frame and an excellent sense of timing to hold the children spellbound with his villainy.'

1964 March 12th
A Man Dies by Ewan Hooper and Ernest Marvin
I have spoken of this in another part of the book. The impact made when we did this play remains with us yet. We are contemplating doing it again. We would like to take this production on tour, if we could get a sufficient number of bookings to make it worth-while.

1964 April 29th–May 2nd
The Tinder Box by Nicholas Stuart Gray
Again this play came over with éclat. Many of the audience thought it the best we had done for a long time. One gentle-

man said the production showed a degree of excellence which seemed to crystallize all the past excellence of the Theatre. We felt very proud at such a tribute.

1964　November 23rd–28th
Richard III by William Shakespeare

In honour of Shakespeare's 400th anniversary we gave seven performances of this play. I had hoped that it would be the best Shakespeare we had ever done. Actually I was disappointed. I was short of older boys, and had appealed to several schools with dismal results. The one or two boys who did step in to help worked valiantly, but were not strong enough. I was not ashamed of the production, but disappointed. The first night was a Gala performance, with the Mayor and Mayoress as host and hostess. The Mayor, Councillor William Fernhead, JP, welcoming the guests, touched on the poor support the Theatre gets in the borough. His remarks caused some annoyance among certain people. It seems a pity that when someone tries to help there is always someone upset.

His remarks did some good and we were very grateful. On listening to conversations in the refreshment bar on the opening night I sadly came to the conclusion that it is little use trying to do serious drama for the general public. They will not try to assimilate it.

I had several messages of appreciation from the few discriminating members of the audiences. I personally was very thrilled by the performances of quite a few of the cast, particularly the girls. They were superb.

1965　January 27th–30th
The Imperial Nightingale by Nicholas Stuart Gray

This was another repeat and we were proved fully justified in doing it again. Good audiences revelled in the mysterious atmosphere. The delightful sets carried us away to the land of Mandarins. This is the sort of play where young artists find just the type of characters that can give scope to their natural talent. Youth owes a great debt to Nicholas Stuart Gray.

1965   March 14th

'Apart from producing a regular flow of well-acted plays, a good deal of controversy, a film star and theatre conscious-ness among local young people, Stretford Children's Theatre can now add a young playwright to its list of achievements.

'He is Andrew Winton, who has been with the Children's Theatre for five years, and has displayed an acting talent rare on the amateur stage.

'He has frequently taken the lead in the Theatre's produc-tions, notably their brilliant production of *Richard III* last year, which was a personal triumph for Andrew. But he has had a host of minor parts, sometimes two or three in one play, an indication of his versatility.

'Andrew is now in charge of rehearsals for his first play, *Funny, Isn't It?*'

Stretford Journal

1965   May 19th–22nd
The Stone Cage by Nicholas Stuart Gray

This was a new play to us and we had much pleasure in its preparation. Our scenery and effects departments were kept busy. Here again our lighting, so important in fantasy plays, was really first class. We sometimes get the most amazing effects with some bits of cardboard, a spotlight and an in-telligent child. When we achieve one of these indescribable moments, I am sure the thrill is just as great as coming up on the pools. I would rather be blessed with imagination than have the wealth of the Indies without it.

1965   October 13th–16th
Twelfth Night by William Shakespeare

We managed to achieve a rollicking pace in this production. A simple set, colourful costumes and some high spots of comedy made it a memorable show. Feste was outstanding.

It is a tribute to the hard work of all sections of the Theatre that the only item hired was Sir Andrew Aguecheek's wig. Another pleasurable feature was—we had good houses.

1965   December 8th–11th
The Young Dick Whittington by Alan Broadhurst

This is a delightful play, ideal for youth groups. It has an uncomplicated story; the element of mime is a source of inspiration. We revelled in every moment of it—and so did the audience.

The Manchester Comet said this about our show, 'In movement his actors and actresses excel. The arrest of Spree, Farquharson and Hodge by the Press Gang was the most finely planned and executed scuffle scene I have seen in amateur theatre in Manchester.'

In December 1960, the *Stretford Journal* wrote a lengthy article on the work of the Theatre. The writer, Tony Glynn, rounded his remarks with the following paragraphs.

'A teacher at Old Trafford Secondary School for 30 years, Mr Holland handles youth with a persuasive, but sympathetic, way, and it is apparent that he has the gift of passing on his own conviction and feeling to the children.

'In that large house in Talbot Road every night of the week, there gathers a large and joyful family. It is more than an artistic group. It is a friendly social body which helps in its way to develop in children the essential qualities of working together in common harmony to achieve a desirable aim.

'Look into it deeply enough, and you will see that it helps to produce good citizens.'

1966   March 2nd–5th
Heidi by Beryl Jones
adapted from the story by Johanna Spyri

The outstanding feature of our production was the début of two new members in the leading roles. Gay, sensitive Julie Thompson in the leading character was an ideal choice.

The *Manchester Evening News* pinpointed an interesting

and important observation. They said, 'Youngsters brought up on a diet of Daleks and Westerns can still be enchanted by one of the old favourite classics. Spellbound boys and girls at the Stretford Children's Theatre certainly proved this. As well as the delightful story, they were probably fascinated by the fact that the players were, like themselves children— and a talented bunch at that.

The production came over as fresh as a new fall of snow on the Swiss mountains, where the story is set.' This proved a delightfully satisfying show to stage.

1966   April 26th and 27th
Ten Little Niggers by Agatha Christie

This was put on as part of the National Savings Association's Jubilee celebrations. We enjoyed doing it. Once again Andrew Winton gave an outstanding performance, as the maniac judge.

1966   October 12th–15th
The Lord of the Amber Mountain by Derek Lomas

The author sent me the first act of this play to read. I was attracted, and asked for the remaining acts. Having read these I decided to do it. We were the first company to present it, and it was well received.

1966   December 7th–10th
Pinocchio by Brian Way and Warren Jenkins

I know Brian Way personally and I admire his work. I am not a great lover of much audience participation, but I had promised myself I would do this play sometime. I felt it fitted in with the spirit we needed for our Christmas show, so we decided to present it. It proved to be both a financial and artistic success.

Reporting, the *Stretford Journal* said: 'And how the junior audience participated! The "baddies" were roundly booed from the moment they appeared. Tiny fists shook in their direction as they conspired. And when they were chased up and down the aisles by rotund policemen and human blood-hounds many parents had to restrain over-eager offspring obviously bent on making citizens' arrests. An outstanding feature was the excellent masks for Cat and Fox made by Geoffrey Duke, who played Fox.'

1967   March 8th–11th
Othello by William Shakespeare

I chose to present this play for two reasons. It was one of the plays in the 'A' level GCE examination syllabus, and we had always intended including it in our programme. I consider the result was the best all round standard of any play we have produced to date.

Othello was taken by Geoffrey Duke, whose work in the Theatre has improved steadily during the last five seasons. His interpretation was sensitive and impressive. Andrew Winton's Iago was a gem. The Desdemona of sixteen-year-old Christine Hayes was a remarkably mature piece of work. Emilia, Cassio and Roderigo completed a really excellent cast. There were a few weaknesses, but they were definitely minor. I was proud and thrilled at the result. This was a fine ending to a wonderful season. It was a financial loss, but an artistic gain.

The following is typical of letters which appear in the local press from time to time.

'Sir, May I, through your columns thank Mr Holland and all his wonderful workers at the Stretford Children's Theatre for the magnificent production of *The Land of the Christmas Stocking*? What a magnificent show!

'My son likes the theatre but is ridiculed. He hates football, but is forced to play it.

'He joined the Children's Theatre, and enjoys every minute of it. He has improved in every way since he started attending rehearsals. He has found an outlet for his interests and is very happy.

'I am an ardent theatregoer, and I find the productions

of the Stretford Children's Theatre outstandingly satisfying. There is a sincerity and artistic unity about them which is often missing in even professional shows today.

'How ashamed Stretford should be that there is ever an empty seat at these performances. When my son asked his teacher if his classmates could form a party to see this show the reply was, "No, I've no time to bother with such rubbish."

'Well, if Saturday night's performance was rubbish, it's a pity we don't have more of it.

'Keep battling on Mr Holland. There is a growing band of parents who value what your company of wonderful workers are doing. Long may you prosper.

Yours, etc.,

A VERY GRATEFUL PARENT

Stretford.'

O

26

11th July 1963

I cannot write a history of our Theatre without reference to this date. Although I was the sole actor on the stage for this production, and naturally I was filled with pride and overwhelmed with emotion, I never felt anything else but that I, in my person, represented the Theatre from its youngest member to its oldest; from the timid onlooker who had watched when others were doing, to the veteran who has perhaps helped in all the departments of our organization.

The first news of this event arrived on 4th April 1963. I was leaving my form room, en route for the Staff Room and a cup of tea, when my colleague who was on yard duty met me. Handing me a letter, he said, 'I think you must have missed this at nine o'clock.'

Printed on the envelope were the words, 'University of Manchester' and underneath the word 'Confidential' was typewritten.

Thinking it was the normal request for a report on a student who had been doing his teaching practice with us I casually opened it on my way upstairs. I read as follows:

From

The Vice Chancellor,

The University,

Manchester, 13

Confidential   3rd April 1963

Dear Mr Holland,

I have much pleasure in writing to inform you that the

Council and Senate propose to ask the Court of the University, at its meeting on May 15th, to authorize the conferment upon you of the Degree of Master of Arts (honoris causa).

It is proposed that the Degree should be conferred at the Degree Ceremony to be held on the morning of Thursday July 11th. I shall be glad if it is possible for you to make arrangements to keep this date free so that you could be present at the ceremony on the occasion to receive the degree.

Will you kindly regard this information as strictly confidential until the Court has approved the recommendation? As soon as this has been done, I will communicate with you again.

Yours sincerely,
W. Mansfield Cooper

I mean it literally when I say my heart missed a beat. I had never experienced such a shock. The whole thing was as the proverbial bolt from the blue.

My wife was in hospital at the time, having just had an operation. The shock of my news must have appeared on my face, because immediately I entered the Staff Room, my colleagues just stared open-mouthed. One said, 'Have you had bad news from the hospital?'

I was so shaken, that for a moment I did nothing but stand there gasping like a fish. Eventually I managed to blurt out, 'NO, thanks, actually it's not bad news, but very good news.' Naturally they wanted to know what it was. I told them that at the moment I could not satisfy their curiosity, but promised to do so as soon as I was able.

The bell went. I was still standing there bemused. Alan, our Science master said, 'I think I'd sit down a minute.'

He poured out a cup of tea, and handed it to me saying, 'Is it bad news?'

I looked at him and said, 'Well, I know you can keep a secret, and if I don't tell someone, I think I'll burst.' I handed the letter to him.

Silently he read it, then thrusting out his hand, he heartily shook mine, saying as he did so, 'Well, recognition at last!'

Naturally, that night, when I broke the news to my wife, she was overjoyed. We could not really believe it.

Of course I was proud of the great honour, but what thrilled me most was the public acknowledgement of the value of the work of Children's Theatre. This fact made the whole thing stupendous. I was agog to tell my fellow workers, and the children, but this had to wait.

In due course I received the confirmatory letter and the news leaked out. The first public mention came on the evening of May 15th. It was the opening night of *The Snow Queen*. When the press came to discuss the play at the first interval, one of the reporters offered his congratulations, saying they had received news of the award just before he had left the offices of the paper. I was able to tell my colleagues and the cast that evening.

I was overwhelmed by telephone messages, personal calls, letters, postcards and telegrams. I was very deeply touched by these manifestations of joy in my good fortune.

One of my friends, meeting a councillor, asked the latter if he did not consider this bit of news wonderful, received the answer, 'Oh yes, but it makes one wonder if Mr Holland neglects his job.' Ah, well, such is the world.

Our school was given a day's holiday on July 11th. For once I was very popular.

The ceremony itself was an unforgettable experience. I was allowed to have a small party of friends to watch the proceedings. I invited some of my friends who had been closely associated with me in the Theatre, in the Educational world, and in the Chester Diocese, where for many years I had lectured at summer schools. Among these friends I included one of the school prefects, David Ward, who was also a member of the Theatre.

I was presented to the late Lord Woolton, the Chancellor of the University, by Professor R. A. C. Oliver, Sarah Fielden Professor of Education, and Director of the Department of Education at Manchester University, who, on presentation made the following speech, which I think is more than worthy to be included here.

'My Lord Chancellor,

'Here is a teacher, a man of whom Browning might have been prophetically writing in The Pied Piper of Hamelin

> "*He advanced to the Council table;*
> *And, 'Please your honours,' said he, 'I'm able*
> *By means of a secret charm to draw*
> *All creatures living beneath the sun*
> *After me as you never saw.'* "

'The children of Stretford who follow him could say with the child in the poem:

> "*He led us to a joyous land,*
> *Joining the town, and just at hand.*"

His "secret charm" is his love of children and the theatre. Like the Pied Piper, he has been somewhat stinted of guilders but this has not daunted the creator of the Stretford Children's Theatre. By means of financial expedients neglected on Broadway and in the West End, such as Bring and Buy Sales, Beetle Drives, and the vending of tuck, he has contrived to run his Theatre with less resounding losses than many a metropolitan theatre manager, and at a higher artistic profit than some.

'He has an eye for talent, and some of his juvenile players have gone on to distinguish themselves on the professional boards. But he is not dependent on the genius of the born actor, he discovers, nay, creates talent in the ordinary boy or girl. To his children "the play's the thing", "they have their exits and their entrances", and blossoming in the warmth of his enthusiasm, "in the two hours' traffic of the stage", young boys and girls are level now with men.

'His family of three hundred children is a happy one, but they are not more happy than he. He needs, my Lord, no reward, for with him love's labour is not lost; but we would give ourselves the satisfaction of honouring him.

'My Lord, and Chancellor, on behalf of the University I present to you, Bert Holland for the degree of Master of Arts, honoris causa.'

As Professor Oliver put my hand into that of the Lord Chancellor, I could not have uttered a word had I been required to do so.

Lord Woolton shook my hand, and in a few well-chosen words, welcomed me into the ranks of the distinguished; I could not see him for the mist which descended. I murmured my thanks, bowed, and stumbled down the steps back to my seat. I was only faintly conscious of the acclamation accorded to me as I sat down. Never in my life before had I been so deeply affected.

It was most interesting to me that another recipient of an Honorary Degree with me that day was another theatre lover. He had also founded a theatre though of another kind. This was Mr (now Sir) Nicholas Thomas Sekers, who founded a silk mill and the Rosehill Theatre Trust in Cumberland.

The general attitude of my colleagues and the people in Stretford, who had known me many years, was of pleasure. The world being what it is, certain people openly expressed disapproval. This attitude will, I fear, always be present when something pleasant happens. I can never understand why such people prefer to coin discord rather than circulate happiness.

I have never ceased to marvel at the honour bestowed upon me by the University of Manchester. It is my proudest possession.

When I see the delight shining on the faces of the cast when they are totally absorbed in a production, I thank God the theatre has been instrumental in fanning the flame of their spiritual perceptiveness. To have been granted the opportunity to do this is a great reward for all the effort we have made in this jungle world.

27

1945—66

On 26th April 1966, our Theatre was twenty-one years old. There was a mention in the press. Our local *Stretford Journal* noted it, and reference was made to it on Sunday, June 12th, on the BBC, in Spectrum.

On our actual birthday, April 26th, we opened our production of *Ten Little Niggers*, which we performed for the Stretford Savings Association, as part of their Jubilee Celebrations.

Their Chairman, Mrs N. Horner, presented us with a large cake made by a member of the Savings Committee. At the first interval, Mrs Horner proposed the toast of the Theatre, which we drank in tea, and Miss Blodwyn Williams cut the cake.

The cast had had a whip-round, and presented me with something a little stronger than tea, with which to drink to the continuing success of the Theatre.

As a coming of age gesture, at our April Executive Committee Meeting, a very important decision was made. I had hoped we could do just this, as the next step on our journey, and to my deep satisfaction, we inaugurated a Building Fund. Personally this gave me the greatest happiness. To know this fund is actually started is a wonderful satisfaction.

When Andrew Winton presented me with the gift on the evening of 26th April, he handed me a cheque for five pounds, the first donation to our Building Fund.

I realize that, repeating the attitude prevalent in 1945 when we founded the Theatre, many people will consider our ambition little short of madness. I do not think it is. Faith can remove mountains. We have faith. The mountains are there. We must just prove the statement.

We are not given to know the exact extent of our earthly sojourn, so I do not know how long I have ahead of me to continue my exertions. What I do know is that, given reasonable health, I shall fight for our aims as long as I have a breath in my body.

At the moment I have no detailed idea as to how much we require to build this theatre. It must not be a second-rate, makeshift type of building. It must be the best. I have been looking at all kinds of plans recently. There have been several theatres built in England and abroad for amateur groups since the last war. I would say, at a rough guess, we would require a minimum of fifty thousand pounds, but in order to have the whole organization on a footing which would ensure the best work, I have the sum of seventy-five thousand pounds at the back of my mind.

I am praying earnestly that some wealthy persons who love the arts will look kindly on our efforts, and, learning of our struggles over twenty-one years, may have the urge to help us. Cheques from wealthy patrons would be marvellous, but I think that seventy-five thousand people each sending a donation of one pound would release such a strong force of goodwill that nothing could then stop us doing what we are aiming to do.

In 1963, £866 million were spent on various gambling pursuits in the British Isles. The cost of the World Cup matches read in millions. Thousands are spent every year in building sports' stadiums. Patrons of these schemes seldom grumble at the cost. Is it too much to ask that a few thousands be diverted to our cause?

We have made a second plan to commemorate our coming of age. At the moment we are rehearsing six short plays to take on tour. Our idea is that churches, chapels, schools or any interested body provide the venue, do the advertising and get the audiences together. We will supply the play.

All the expenses are paid out of the takings, and the profit is shared between the organization accepting our services and ourselves. It is full steam ahead to make the first thousand for our Building Fund.

Thanks to the generosity of our Chairman we shall be having a Celebration Dinner, when we hope to have some well-known theatrical personality as our guest speaker.

28

The British Children's
Theatre Association

This organization was founded at Easter 1959. A meeting of people known to be interested in all forms of theatre for children and adolescents was convened in Leicester by Mr Michael Pugh.

This event was most exciting to me personally. To realize that at last the few pockets of activity dealing with children's theatre in different parts of the country, where young people were being introduced to good live theatre, were going to have the opportunity to unite and further their common aim was a thrilling prospect.

After a few days' exciting, illuminating discussions The British Children's Theatre Association was formed, and the Committee set about formulating a constitution, which has constantly been improved during the last seven years.

I would say that the hard work put in by the committee members of this organization has resulted in what must be one of the most successful organizations in the country. This serious attention to the aims of the Association by a small band of dedicated people has resulted in help and encouragement to all who work in the field of theatre for the young.

The aims of the Association are as follows: the purpose of The British Children's Theatre Association shall be to further education for children through drama and the arts of the theatre, and to encourage the appreciation of dramatic art for children, and as a ancillary thereto the following subsidiary purposes:

1. To undertake and publish the results of research into methods of educating children through drama and the arts of the theatre.
2. To promote all aspects of educational drama, and the arts of the theatre for children in schools, colleges, universities and theatre Companies.
3. To encourage municipal authorities to build regional educational centres with facilities for drama for children.
4. To do all such other matters or things as may appear to the Association in General Meeting to be incidental or conducive to the attainment of the above-mentioned objects, or any of them.
5. To provide varied opportunities for those interested in children's theatre to meet to discuss the problems peculiar to it.
6 To encourage the habit of theatre-going among children and young people, and to help to foster the arts of the theatre by developing an audience of the future.
7. To encourage the writing of children's theatre plays, and to persuade publishing houses to accept them.
8. To compile and maintain a Bibliography of recommended plays, and to make known the availability of those plays, and other suitable acting material.
9. To be prepared to advise, and seek advice on children's theatre matters, and to maintain contact with organizations at home and abroad.
10. To produce and maintain a Directory of all children's theatres in the country.

There are three types of membership:

1. *Group Membership*
   This is open to Amateur Children's Theatres. The annual subscription for this type of membership is three guineas.

2. *Individual Membership*

This is open to anyone interested in Children's Theatre, and the annual subscription is one guinea.

3. *Associate Membership*

This section is for Professional children's theatres, which receive an invitation from the Association.

Invitations are restricted to those theatres using an Esher Contract.

The annual subscription is two guineas.

All members are entited to:

1. An invitation to the Annual Children's Theatre Conference.
2. The Directory of Children's Theatres
3. The Bibliography of plays recommended for performance by Children's Theatres.
4. The Newsletter of the Association.
5. A list of members.

Anyone who is interested in joining this organization should contact the Secretary:

Gerald Tyler,
County Education Offices,
Bond Street,
Wakefield.
Yorks.

The President of the Association is:

The Lord Willis.

The Vice President is:

Dame Sybil Thorndike, DBE, (Lady Casson).

Chairman:

Clifford Williams,
Royal Shakespeare Theatre,
Stratford-upon-Avon.

In conversation, Mr Gerald Tyler said:

'The Association is broadly based in the theatre and in education, because its members do not see children's theatre merely in terms of presentation whether amateur or professional, but rather as a question of what the arts and theatre arts in particular can do to enrich the child by widening his horizons, developing his creativity and awakening his love of the arts.

'It is therefore difficult for them to separate entirely what the child sees from what the child does as they are both important parts of the same experience. This makes children's theatre a combined operation in which different facets of the community can play their parts. It is the place where the professional theatre person and the professional educationist meet and play equally valuable parts, and where the influence of the home and the cultural social life of the community must be taken into account.

'This means that the membership is culled from the theatre and from education, and from persons interested in children's theatre in its broadest interpretation—actors, teachers, dancers, puppeteers, lecturers, professors, librarians, Local Education Authorities, Colleges of Education writers, Arts Associations, and others. Television, puppetry, opera and ballet have all a part to play.

'It is right that persons eminent in their fields of work have joined the Association. The majority of the existing professional companies organized to perform children's theatre are members. Strong support is given by the National Association of Drama Advisers.

'The Education Drama Association has reciprocal representation with the Educational Puppetry Association and Laban Art of Movement Guild.

'In 1964 the Association held an International Conference at the Commonwealth Institute, London. This was a momentous assembly, where some thirty-five nations were represented. Each evening we saw a performance of children's theatre plays given by British and foreign companies.'

I would draw special attention to the section of the Association dealing with the encouragement of the writing of suitable plays for child audiences. There is an urgent demand for good plays of the nature, and the panel dealing with original plays is very keen to receive manuscripts for consideration. Any play of real merit stands a good chance of being produced by one of the children's theatre groups in the country Further, if it succeeds in pleasing the child audience, it will most likely achieve publication.

No one who is genuinely interested in theatre for youth can afford to be outside the ranks of the British Children's Theatre Association, if they want their interest kept alive and stimulated.

I am proud to be a founder-committee member. We have very ambitious, far-reaching schemes in embryo to help children's theatre to advance to where it ought to be in the life of the nation.

STRETFORD CHILDREN'S THEATRE

Income and Expenditure Account for year ended 31st December 1964

EXPENDITURE	£ s. d.	£ s. d.	INCOME	£ s. d.
To Hon. Secretary's Expenses		11 12 4	By Donations: Stretford Corporation	200 0 0
Hon. Treasurer's Expenses		2 0 0	Others	14 12 6
Hon. Registrar's Expenses		4 18 11	Patrons	59 6 0
Printing and Stationery		22 15 6	Subscriptions	20 3 0
Producer's Expenses		5 0 0	Sale of Scrap Lead	5 15 6
Bank Interest and Charges		3 8 6	B.B.C. Fee	15 15 0
Subscriptions—Children's Theatre Assoc.		3 3 0	Special Efforts	244 18 3
Income Tax on Interest received		8 10 6	Hire of Costumes	44 0 0
Headquarters Expenses—			Programme Advertising	12 10 0
Ground Rent	16 18 8			£617 0 3
Repairs and Cleaning	1189 14 3			
Insurances	11 14 0			
Rates	14 1 6			
Electricity	87 10 7		Excess of Expenditure over Income	
Gas	24 10 4		for the year	£893 14 9
Water	7 4 0			
General	2 17 9			
		1354 11 1		
Coffee Bar				
Expenses	71 7 7			
Instalments on Record Player	17 3 6			
	88 11 1			
Less: Income	50 10 0	38 1 1		
Productions				
Expenses	470 11 11			
Less: Income	413 17 10	56 14 1		
		£1510 15 0		£1510 15 0

Balance Sheet as at 31st December 1964

	£ s. d.	£ s. d.		£ s. d.
Income and Expenditure Account			Land and Buildings, 28 Talbot Road at cost	1089 10 0
Balance as at 1st January, 1964	1528 1 9		less proceeds of sale	
Less: Excess of Expenditure over			Costumes	15 13 9
Income for the year 1964	893 14 9	634 7 0	Cash in hands of Hon. Treasurer	14 2 4
Hilda Donigan Memorial Fund		7 17 0		
Loan		20 0 0		
Sundry Creditors		98 15 2		
Bank Overdraft		358 6 11		
		£1119 6 1		£1119 6 1

HON. AUDITOR'S REPORT

I have examined the above Balance Sheet and Income and Expenditure Account which in my opinion respectively give a true and fair view of the state of the Theatre's affairs as at the 31st December, 1964, and of its income and expenditure for the year ended on that date.

4th June 1965.   S. R. Johnson, Incorporated Accountant, Hon. Auditor.

One of our balance sheets

STRETFORD CHILDREN'S THEATRE

'HEIDI'

**The World Famous Children's Play
By BERYL M. JONES**

At the Civic Theatre,
Chester Road, Stretford on
**Wednesday, Thursday, Friday, and Saturday
MARCH 2, 3, 4, 5**
at 7-15 p.m.
A cordial invitation is extended to you to bring
a party to witness this production.
The charge for admission is 3/6, Children 2/-.
All seats numbered and reserved.
We shall be pleased to send you 1 adult 3/6 ticket free
for every 10 tickets booked.
Kindly fill in the attached form and send it to me as
quickly as possible.
Miss B. M. WILLIAMS, Business Manager.

•••

To Miss B. M. Williams,
58 Shrewsbury Street, Old Trafford, Manchester 16.
Telephone TRA 2986

Please forward............................tickets at 3/6..................... at 2/-
for "HEIDI"
on..

Cheque/Postal Order for ....enclosed.

Name ....

Address ....

Representing ....

Sent out to schools with handbills

29

Professional Children's Theatres

Educated, cultured and thoughtful people throughout the country have, for some considerable time, tried to find ways and means to give young people an opportunity to see good, live theatre.

Quite a number of professional groups started, worked hard for a few years, lost money, and then reluctantly had to retire from the field.

Why are we so blind in England? In other countries Children's Theatres are subsidized to the tune of thousands of pounds per annum, yet in this country, still, with all its faults, just about the finest in the world, we ignore our artistic heritage. We prefer to build sports' stadiums, allow unhealthy beat cellars, and dubious strip-tease clubs to flourish.

Some outstanding names like Esmé Church, John Allen, John English, and the late George Devine, all recall noble efforts to bring good theatre to young people. They all had to give up their theatres, because it became financially impossible to continue. We owe them deep gratitude.

One theatre which has managed to flourish is Miss Bertha Waddell's Scottish Children's Theatre. It certainly deserves its success. Miss Waddell was awarded the MBE for her work with her Theatre the same year I was awarded my honour.

There are a few dedicated people who are struggling at the present time to keep companies presenting plays for young people functioning. With them it is becoming in-

P

creasingly more difficult, and some already are threatened with extinction, unless financial aid is forthcoming.

One of the best known is The Unicorn Theatre for Children, under the direction of the dedicated Caryl Jenner, which was founded in 1948. Its main aim is to bring a true experience of theatre to young audiences and to provide experiences which will remain with them long after the performance is over.

It has had one or two small grants, but if no subsidy is available before the end of this year, then this wonderful little theatre will have to close. At the present time, thirty-six performers, making up four companies, give over seven hundred performances per year, playing to 200,000 children.

In conversation, Miss Jenner said, 'Financially it is impossible to achieve all we know we can at present, but what we do know is that given *good* plays, *good* actors, *good* direction, *good* designers and *good* conditions, the true experience of theatre at the highest level can be achieved.'

It is exhilarating to meet with such sincere enthusiasm as one encounters in the world of children's theatre. None is more dedicated and enthusiastic than Mr Alwyn D. Fox, Director of the Westminster Theatre Children's Theatre. The 1965–66 season was the busiest ever for this very fine company.

Mr Fox shares with me the belief that we cannot gauge the capacity for enjoyment of the average child. He can tell many anecdotes to support this view from the experiences of his company on their travels around the country. This last season they have visited the West country, the South of England, the Outer London area, and as far north as Lancashire, playing to all types of schools. An interesting invitation came one recent season from Dorothy Lady Henley to give a special performance at Walton Court for the children from surrounding villages.

The 1966 summer engagement under the Greater London Council is the fourth consecutive season for this civic body. No more dedicated company treads the boards.

Anyone interest in Laban technique should certainly see a performance by the British Dance Drama Theatre under the direction of Gerard Bagley.

The policy of this theatre is to support the teaching of movement, creative drama, dance and mime through lecture-demonstrations and fully staged performances by professional artists and qualified teachers.

Completely different programmes are presented for Infant, Junior, and Secondary Schools, combining song, speech, dance and music. Each programme embodies an amusing demonstration of their guiding principles that involve audience participation. They are always colourfully costumed and possess their own lighting equipment, drapes and sound equipment. A stage is not essential for their kind type of production. The company is sponsored annually by the Greater London Council and other Education Associations. I can thoroughly recommend this group of very clever artists.

Another excellent company is The London Children's Theatre. This is under the direction of another pioneer in presenting good plays to young people, Mr Brian Way. He has worked unceasingly for years with great success. He aims to provide opportunities for experiment and research into the forms of theatre most suitable for children.

He aims to assist teachers in all types of schools with a method of approach to drama in education, and to encourage among children an interest in and appreciation of the living theatre.

A branch of drama which appeals strongly to children is puppetry. An excellent example of good puppetry can be seen in a performance of the Lilliput Marionette Theatre, directed by Bernard C. Lewis. This Theatre presents plays through the medium of marionettes, with 'live' voices. Audiences are shown the methods of manipulation, and questions concerning puppetry are answered without reservation. Children are encouraged to regard puppetry as equal to other forms of dramatic art.

Surely no one who is interested in Children's Theatre can be ignorant of that truly wonderful book *Child Drama* by Peter Slade. Peter Slade is probably the most outstanding pioneer in drama work for young people. Actor, producer, BBC announcer, 'Uncle', writer, lecturer, he is a moving spirit behind many unique ventures in the world of drama.

In 1937 he founded an Arts Centre in Worcestershire. Emotionally disturbed children were sent to him, and through drama he achieved wonderful remedial results that were shown to the medical profession in London. He worked closely with psychoanalysts. He then enlisted in the army, and was blown up when filming bomb disposal work and invalided out of the army.

Since 1947 Peter Slade has been Drama Adviser for Birmingham where he has done so much excellent work as Director of the Educational Drama Association. He founded Birmingham Experimental Drama Centre where adults and children come for training in theatre. Centres have been founded as far afield as Canada where his methods have been used with outstanding success. Each year he conducts Educational Drama Association Summer Schools.

My first meeting with Peter was some years ago when I strongly disagreed with him across the floor of a meeting in London. Since working with him now for six years on the committee of the British Children's Theatre Association I have come greatly to admire him, his sincerity and his achievements. I revere him for his great love and understanding of children, and am proud to call him my friend.

There are other well-known professional children's theatres, but I mention these because I am personally acquainted with their work, and can honestly recommend all of them.

I append the addresses of these theatres at the end of this chapter.

The professional adult theatre is at last waking up to the fact that they can do a great deal to aid and encourage the training of young people in the way of enjoying theatre. The

Royal Shakespeare Theatre, Stratford-upon-Avon, The Belgrade Theatre, Coventry, The Sheffield Playhouse, The Nottingham Playhouse and many Repertory Theatres are experimenting successfully in catering for youth, by trying all kinds of new and exciting schemes. I foresee this work growing. It is impossible to express the thrill one experiences on learning of these developments. Even some local councils are showing genuine inclination to help. We pioneers must not relax but redouble our efforts.

The Scottish Children's Theatre
    Director Bertha Waddell, MBE,
        Caldergrove House,
        Cambuslang,
        Lanarkshire.

Unicorn Children's Theatre
    Director Caryl Jenner,
        2 Warwick Close,
        London, W.8.

Westminster Children's Theatre
    Director Alwyn D. Fox,
        1 Hogarth Terrace,
        London, W.4.

British Dance Drama Theatre.
    Director Gerard Bagley,
        2 Melbourne Road,
        Wimbledon,
        London, SW.19.

London Children's Theatre
    Director Brian Way,
        34 South Molton Street
        London, W.1.

Lilliput Marionette Theatre
  Director Bernard C. Lewis,
    31 Avondale Road,
    Wolverhampton.

Educational Drama Association Children's Theatre Players
  Director Peter Slade,
    The Drama Centre,
    Red Street South,
    Birmingham.

Note: The Education Drama Association Children's Theatre Players are not professionals, but trained amateurs. Their work over several years has been so unique that I mention them because I think anyone who is genuinely interested in children's theatre should certainly know of their existence, and, if possible, see some of their work.

30

Bibliography

I have produced, seen or read all the following plays, and can thoroughly recommend them as eminently suitable for child or youth audiences.

Much learned discussion takes place and many heated words fly about, concerning what plays the teenager likes. I once again reiterate my view that we do not know in very great detail to what the young intellect and emotions react.

The young audience loves fantasy, the bright world of magic and charm, as it always has done and ever will do, unless we smother it at birth by choking it with petrol fumes and inoculating it with the yearning for wealth before it has had a chance to see the glory of the earth. Adventure, tenderness and, yes, tragedy will never fail to strike a responsive reflection in the heart of a child.

The teenager, in the main, likes much the same as the adult today. Do not let us imagine that because youth has a hard, brittle, brash exterior, which after all is only a mirror of life as it is, it cannot appreciate the romance just round the corner. Test it and see.

The British Children's Theatre Association publication *Selected Bibliography of Plays Recommended for Performance to Child Audiences* is excellent. It is on sale to members and non-members, price two shillings and sixpence, postage sixpence, from the Secretary.

I have not mentioned those plays which are in the chapter entitled 'Our Record', as the comments on these will indicate the type of plays they **are**.

Because the following are recommended for Juniors it

does not mean that older children and adults would not enjoy them.

Where do we go from Here? by Helga Burgess
This is published by MacDonald and Young. The royalty is on a sliding scale.

It is an attractive fairy-tale, and lasts one and a quarter hours. The cast is infinitely variable. There are eight sets, but I have seen it effectively played to curtains. Costumes are present day, and various national.

It was very successfully produced at the Edinburgh Festival.

Hans, the Witch and the Goblin by Alan Cullen
Published by Samuel French, Scripts four shillings. Royalty four guineas.

It is an original fairy-tale with two interior and one exterior sets. Cast: 7 males, four females, two pigs. Costumes are fairy-tale. It plays for two hours.

The Puppet Prince by Michael Drin
Published by Curtis Brown. Royalty 7 per cent. It lasts for two and a half hours.

This play, one of intrigue, was successfully produced at the Library Theatre, Johannesburg.

Cast: 7 males, 4 females, a parrot and a mouse.

Niccolo and Nicolette by Alan Cullen
Published by the Children's Theatre Press.

This original fairy-tale plays for two hours.

Cast: 6 males, 3 females, a cockerel and extras.

Royalty: five guineas. Scripts: eight shillings.

The Glass Slipper by Eleanor and Herbert Farjeon
Published by Samuel French. Royalty by arrangement.
Scripts four shillings.

It is a fairy-tale musical, and plays two and a half hours.
Sets: four interior, four exterior.
Cast: 8 males, 12 females, dancers, extras.

The Proud Princess by Mary Howarth
Copies of scripts from the authoress. Royalty by arrangement.
This is a fairy story, with nursery rhymes set to music that plays two and a half hours. It is written for large cast, but can be done with a smaller cast.
Sets: 6 exterior, 2 interior.

Listen to the Wind by Angela Jeans
Music by Vivian Ellis. Published by Samuel French. Libretto seven shillings. Royalty by arrangement.
A musical-fairy tale, it plays for two hours.
Cast: 20 varied characters. 9 scenes.

Where the Rainbow Ends by Clifford Mills and John Ramsey
Published by Samuel French. Royalty by arrangement.
Music is available, but it can be played without.
This fairy-tale plays for two and a half hours.
Cast: any number over twenty.
Sets: 1 interior, 6 exterior.

The Poppencast by Antonia Ridge
Published by Faber. Royalty by arrangement.
A folk tale, it plays one hour.
Cast: 9 males, 3 females, Costume: Dutch.
Sets: 1 interior, 2 exterior.

Pinocchio by Brian Way and Warren Jenkins
Published by Dobson. Royalty: two guineas. Script: five shillings.
A fairy-tale, it plays for two hours.
Cast: 15 males, 6 females.
Arena. Opportunites for audience participation.

The Wizard of Oz by Adèle Thone. Based on a story by
L. Frank Baum
Published by the Children's Theatre Press.

Royalty: three and a half guineas. Script: eight shillings.

It plays about two hours. Cast: 11 males, 7 females, but interchangeable.

Sets: 6 interior, 1 exterior. Can be simple.

Greensleeves' Magic by Marian Jonson
Published by Garnet Millar, for the Coach House Press, Inc.

Royalty by arrangement.

It is a medieval folk tale and lasts for one hour.

Cast: 6 males, 5 females.

Set: Garden.

The Enchanted Forest by Anthony Woodhall
Published by Margaret Ramsey. Royalty by arrangement.

It is a fairy-tale and plays two hours.

Cast: 10 males, 10 females, extras.

Sets: 1 interior, 3 exterior.

Should you be particularly interested in plays for Junior and Infant audiences, I would recommend strongly the plays written by Patrick Mace, published by MacDonald and Young.

Two of them, *The Silver Whistle*, and *Jasell*, are prize-winning entries in National Playwriting Competitions. They are all charming, attractive pieces and have rightly earned Patrick Mace success as a writer of children's plays. They reveal the deep understanding of children which he displays in his charming personality.

Particulars of these plays are as follows.

The Silver Whistle

The possession of a magic whistle is very exciting, but it can become extremely tiresome. It turns out to be rather nice to have an ordinary whistle after all.

Playing time: approximately one and a half hours.
Thirteen characters and extras.
Semi-arena presentation. Audience participation.

Jasell

The king is taken ill and the Court Jester, a grotesque clown,
is given brief authority to rule the kingdom. He shows that it
takes a wise man to be a fool.

Playing time approximately one and a quarter hours.
Ten characters and extras.

No Memorial

Eyam in the Plague year.

Suitable for older children.

Playing time approximately one hour.

Costumes 1665

Seven characters and extras.

Cake for the King

Fantastic adventure. Robbers, dragon, hidden treasure and
a cake so light that all who eat a piece float in the air.

Playing time approximately one and a quarter hours.

Audience participation.

Eleven characters and extras.

The Tree and the Fountain

Only the silent stranger entering the town knows how to
make the fountain flow again and the withered tree bear
its precious golden apples, but she cannot speak.

With music, mime and much help from the audience she
finds a way to aid her friends.

Playing time approximately one hour.

Eleven characters and extras.

Harlequin Lends a Hand

An imaginative Commedia del 'Arte play for children, with
Harlequin, Pierrot, Columbine, Pantaloon and others in a

plot concerning stolen jewels and gold.

Playing time approximately forty minutes.

No formal setting.

Ten characters.

The Witch Queen

Original fairy story.

The village is bewitched and must sleep by day and work by night until the spell is broken.

Playing time approximately one hour

No formal setting.

Audience participation.

Eleven characters.

Mr Mace is busy writing more plays. His popularity will, I am sure, grow.

Particulars of royalties, which are very reasonable can be had by writing to the publishers:

> Messrs. Macdonald and Young,
> Youth Dept.,
> Emanwye House,
> Bernard Street,
> London, W.C.1.

The following list of books will be of interest to anyone who is involved in drama at all. Basic procedure in production is the same whether one is dealing with child, youth or adult drama.

I have read every one of these books at one time or another over a period of many years. Each has contributed to my knowledge and personal benefit in some way. Whilst not always agreeing with some of the authors, I nevertheless gained ideas from them all.

Teaching Drama, by Richard Courtney. Published Cassell, 1965. Price 15s.

Child Drama, by Peter Slade. Published U.L.P., 1954. Price 32s. 6d.

Drama for Youth, by Richard Courtney. Published Pitman, 1964. Price 25s.

Leap to Life, by John Wiles and Alan Garrard. Published Chatto and Windus, 1957. Price 15s.

Modern Educational Dance, by Rudolf Laban. Published MacDonald and Evans. Price 10s.

Practical Miming, by Gertrude Pickersgill. Published Pitman, 1935. Price 17s. 6d.

Mime in Schools and Clubs, by Grace Brown. Published MacDonald and Evans. Price 17s. 6d.

Speech and Drama, by Rose Bruford. Published Methuen, 1948. Price 10s. 6d.

Stage Properties and How to Make Them, by Warren Kenton. Published Pitman, 1964. Price 25s.

Planning for New Forms of Theatre, by Stephen Joseph. Published Strand Electric, 1962. Price Gratis.

Drama in Schools, by E. J. Burton. Published Jenkins, 1955. Price 7s. 6d.

Stage Lighting, by Frederick Bentham. Published Pitman, 1955. Price 35s.

The Oxford Companion to the Theatre, by Phyllis Hartnoll. Published O.U.P., 1958. Price 3 gns.

From Story into Drama, by Enid Barr. Published Heinemann Educational Books. Price 16s.

Shakespeare and the Young Actor, by Guy Boas. Published Rockliffe, 1955. Price 21s.

Theatre and Stage. Edited by H. Downs. Published Pitman, 1935. Price Two volumes 4 gns.

Choosing and Producing a Play, by M. H. Fuller. Published Pitman, 1947. Price 4s.

The Art and Science of Stage Management, by P. Goffin. Published J. G. Miller. Price 12s. 6d.

Shakespearean Production, by G. Wilson Knight. Published Faber 1964. Price 2 gns.

Staging a Play, by Nora Lambourne. Published Studio Publication, 1956. Price 18s,

Approach to Theatre for Student Producers, by F. Mackenzie. Published French, 1957. Price 5s.

Musical Production, by L. Mackinlay. Published Jenkins, 1955. Price 7s. 6d.

The Producer and the Play, by N. Marshall. Published Macdonald, 1957. Price 35s.

The Complete Guide to Amateur Dramatics, by Harald Melvill. Published Rockliff, 1957. Price 25s.

Directed Drama, by D. C. Pethybridge. Published U.L.P., 1951. Price 6s.

Producing Plays, by C. B. Purdom. Published Dent, 1951. Price 10s.

Producing Shakespeare, by C. B. Purdom. Published Pitman, 1950. Price 18s.

Music in the Theatre, by R. Settle. Published Jenkins, 1957. Price 7s.

The Open Stage, by R. Southern. Published Faber, 1953. Price 12s. 6d.

The Musical Production, by C. Turfery and K. Palmer. Published Pitman, 1953. Price 30s.

Scene Painting, by R. Forman. Published Pitman, 1950. Price 16s.

Theatre Directory, by Roy Stacey. Published Stacey Publications. Price 2s.

The Story of the Theatre, by J. B. Priestly. Published Rathbone Books. Price 21s.

There are now many publishers who deal with plays for children's theatre, and more playwrights are writing plays for this market.

Samuel French has many suitable plays in their Guide to Selecting Plays, Part V. This is available, post paid, on application. Most educational publishers deal with plays suitable for schools, youth clubs and similar groups, though on reading through some of their lists, I wonder who chooses their selection. Often they are of poor quality.

In fairness I must admit that, now more interest is being

shown in youth theatre, the quality is improving. Macdonald and Young have paid increasing attention to the requirements of the drama enthusiast during the last few years. Another publisher who is doing some excellent work for youth theatre is J. Garnet Miller. He attends the British Children's Theatre Association Conference each year personally, and displays his publications. To be able to chat with a person of his experience and real interest is a great help to a would-be playwright or producer. He publishes a good list of plays suitable for schools and youth clubs. This is available gratis, on request. The address is:

> J. Garnet Miller,
> 13 Tottenham Street,
> London, W.1.

The outstanding firm to publish a long list of excellent plays for children is the Children's Theatre Press of America. These are excellent, having been written by people who have devoted thier lives to the subject of children's theatre. There is now an agency in this country. Their agent is:

> Mrs E. Tyler,
> 'The Oaks',
> Huddersfield Road,
> Brighouse,
> Yorkshire.

Again, a list of publications is available on request, gratis, and Mrs Tyler is always willing to help in choice of plays. Mrs Tyler is also present, with a display of plays and books, at the British Children's Theatre Association Conference each year. You could not do better than contact her about your requirements.

31

J'Accuse

In 1962 when we produced *The Lady's not for Burning*, a local paper printed a leader under the title 'We Accuse'. In this article, the editor asked what the schools were doing to allow a performance of such a standard to be played to such meagre audiences.

Over the years I have, at great trouble, endeavoured to analyse the opposition to, and the disregard of, the Theatre and its work by the people of Stretford and the surrounding districts.

I have come to the conclusion that it can be classed under three headings: utter apathy; ignorance of the Theatre and its aims as carried out in its work; jealousy.

Apathy about the arts among the bulk of the population is without question an established fact. In all districts there is a complete disregard of artistic effort, which, when present, and it does exist in every county, has to be kept alive by the converted few.

Locally, many residents hardly know we exist, and perhaps our name, *Children's* Theatre has not attracted people to our shows. In many minds we are a group of young people cavorting about in the sort of Sunday School entertainment popular at the beginning of this century. We have often been asked to change our name, but like the captain of a ship, I do not like the idea.

One lady said to me recently, 'Candidly, I have no intention of coming to hear Shakespeare murdered by young stars.' It is impossible to reply to such people. They suffer from hardened mental arteries. They are not prepared to go to even one show to see if their sweeping assertion is true. But they do not refrain from condemnation based on complete ignorance. Jealousy is everywhere, whatever the work in hand. What has surprised me is that it has been conspicuous among people whom one would have thought too big to be so niggardly.

In the ranks of the teaching profession there are some of the finest people alive. Selfless, dedicated, undervalued and underpaid, they continue to do their duty and help thousands of young citizens to lead full lives, often without a simple 'thank you' from anyone. It has therefore surprised, disappointed and hurt me to think that much of the opposition we have suffered from has come from people in the education world.

In 1950 we realized that the Theatre was growing so much that it would be impossible for me to fill successfully the roles of both chairman and director. The Executive Committee felt that it would be a good thing for the Theatre to enlist the aid of a well-known local person to act as our chairman. We looked around and thought of various people. Our Education Officer expressed an interest in the post. He was asked and accepted.

He came to a meeting and a few days later I went to see him to discuss certain matters. He informed me that I could not expect the head teachers to support the Theatre unless they were put on the Executive Committee.

As a lover of fair play, I pointed out that when I was contemplating the founding of the Theatre, I had approached head teachers, cap in hand, and been rebuffed. I felt therefore that if they had now changed their minds and wished to join our ranks, the method was very simple. The fairest way from every point of view would be for them to join the Theatre as supporting members, as we all had done, help in whatever department they felt inclined, and then put up their names for election to the Committee at the Annual General Meeting and be voted in. Surely a fair and straight-forward manner. Our new chairman resigned after three months.

Q

When we were looking out for suitable premises for a headquarters, I was taken into the Conservative Club by our Treasurer one Saturday morning. As we sat enjoying a drink, he brought up this subject of a headquarters. He was telling me that he knew of a house owned by the Council, that was empty. He wondered what they intended doing with it. Suddenly he said, 'Why, there's X (pointing to a local worthy) I'll ask him.'

He approached the said gentleman, and said, 'You know that house by the park, belonging to the Council, what are you going to do with it?'

'Why?' was the immediate rejoinder.

'Well, it would make a grand headquarters for the Children's Theatre.'

'We don't want the Children's Theatre to have a head-quarters,' came the spirited reply.

Then the speaker spotted me. His face changed colour like someone flicking through the pages of a coloured bulb catalogue.

I said not a word, but I am human. I would dearly like to know the reason why some of our local people did not want us to have a home.

The late Dr J. Robinson, one of the finest workers for education Stretford has ever had, was for several years the Chairman of the Education Committee. He and Mrs Robinson were for a long time ardent supporters of the Theatre. Suddenly, with no comment, they stopped coming.

I have always believed in going straight to the point. I wrote a letter telling the Doctor that I had heard they were not coming to the Theatre again, and politely asked him if he would kindly give me the reason.

I received a full and courteous reply. Simply put, it was to the effect that someone in the educational world had said that the Theatre was educationally unsound. It taught our youngsters to be precocious, it seduced them from their work and was all in all harmful to them. These are the arguments which are levelled at us by ill-wishers.

I most strongly refute them. Remember I speak after forty-five years' experience in youth drama. Let us look at the accusations, one by one.

Any child will be precocious, IF HE IS ALLOWED TO BE SO. Can you imagine any more precocious child than the little fellow who goes up on the platform on Speech Day to collect an armful of prizes? Or the boy who scores the winning goal? Or the century at cricket? They will all be precocious, IF THEY ARE PERMITTED TO BE SO.

When Mr Percy Lord, the Chief Education Officer for Lancashire, opened our 1962 season, his opening words were, 'Anyone who has the least interest in education should support this venture.'

When we presented one of our musicals with a cast of something like seventy, a lady came to speak to one of our stewards at the end of the performance. Offering a donation and her membership fee, she explained that she had attended several of our shows, and had been trying to make up her mind whether to join or not. That night had decided her. The steward asked her why that was so.

The lady then explained that when the curtain had opened, she saw one little girl of eleven in the chorus, singing as if her life depended on it, with a beatific smile on her face. The family of the little girl was well known to the lady. She said this little girl in the chorus was the only member of her family who had not been in prison. 'If this Theatre can give her such happiness, and keep her out of the hands of the police,' said the lady, 'then it is more than worthy of support.'

A few years ago, a girl of thirteen joined the Theatre. She was rather shy, and chatting to her on the first night she attended at Headquarters, I found out she did not want to act. I introduced her to the youngsters and suggested she brewed the tea ready for tea-break. This she did, and was soon chattering freely and handing round the tea.

About three weeks later, a lady called to see me. Holding out a cheque for a guinea, she said, 'I am not a wealthy person, Mr Holland, but I would like you to accept this for the Theatre with my sincere gratitude for what you have done.' Naturally I asked what this was, as I had no idea to whom I was talking. This was the shy girl's mother. She then told me the story.

Her daughter had been a psychiatric case from an early age and had been under treatment for a considerable time. The father died very suddenly, and the shock to the girl aggravated her condition. Nothing could seem to be done with the girl. She refused to do anything, but just sat there weeping. Her school was powerless to help. The child refused to associate with any other children. She would not read. The mother was nearly demented with anxiety.

Then she had an idea. The girl had seen one or two of our shows. The mother said, 'Would you like to join Mr Holland's Theatre?' The child thought she would.

This girl had been a member for only three weeks and her mother said the change had been amazing. Her daughter was smiling again. She had had some girls from the Theatre to her house for tea. The mother was thrilled at the change.

The psychiatrist who was dealing with the case was full of surprise and admiration. What had we done? Simply given the girl a chance to expand in our friendly atmosphere where young people of her own age were doing something they enjoyed. Later the girl became an active member on the stage, and is still with us, a valuable, energetic, happy unit of our organization. In 1964 the psychiatrist came to see our production of *Julius Caesar*. He sent me a message backstage. 'Tell Mr Holland he does not realize how much good his Theatre is doing.' But, say our detractors, this drama is bad for the children.

The question of homework is easily settled. If a child wishes to work at the Theatre, he will find time to do that and his homework also. I did, and I had a long distance to cycle to school. Both at Headquarters and backstage during the run of a play, we provide space for members to do their homework. It is a common sight to see a boy in Roman outfit or a girl in a crinoline wrestling with quadratic equations!

I recently asked a head teacher who, to the best of my knowledge, has never brought a party to see one of our productions, the reason for this. The reply was revealing. 'The chairs are so hard.' Another head who likewise had very seldom patronized us sent in a booking for nearly a hundred. I was curious to know what had caused the change. When the party arrived at the Theatre, I met the head and expressed my pleasure at seeing them all.

In a manner that made me think of a stiletto dipped in honey, the comment came, 'Well you see, we couldn't get seats at the Library Theatre, so rather than disappoint them we brought them here.' So sweet.

A friend of mine has an aunt—about fifty years of age—who is a teacher. She was bewailing the lack of adventure in our educational methods. My friend then pointed out how the teachers as a whole in the Manchester area had not supported our Theatre. 'Oh,' said the aunt, 'That is understandable. It's not education.'

I think the Archangel Michael would feel annoyed to receive a tap on the back with the words, 'You're doing a grand job, old man. Keep it up,' and then to find the speaker had gone straight off expressly to disparage the work he was doing. To say this is a common experience to all pioneers does not make it less palatable. Nor does it make it right.

I have also noticed that some of the schools who have taken advantage of the various services we provide have not patronized our shows.

On occasions when I have required artists of a certain size or age to fill a cast to my standard, and I have been assured verbally that I could count on full and wholehearted co-operation, it just has not been forthcoming in certain quarters. I frankly admit that there have been other schools which have done everything in their power to help, to our mutual advantage.

After the Mayor's outspoken criticism at the opening

performance of *Richard III* many teachers were offended. I was told a questionnaire was sent out to all schools concerning the work of the Theatre. I was never shown one of these. At that juncture I was asked by a headmaster if I would be willing to meet head teachers to discuss the Theatre. I readily expressed my willingness to do just that. This has never been mentioned to me again. But I will say that the 1965–66 season showed a definite improvement in attendances.

To play to capacity for the four shows that we normally give each production, we would have to sell 1,680 seats. Some individual schools in the district play to over a thousand when school plays are given. Our watershed of potentials should enable us to play two or three weeks if we so desired.

When the Pegasus Theatre of Sheffield give their shows, for a run of three weeks, they are booked to capacity within twenty-four hours. Doncaster Technical College Children's Theatre can play to ten thousand youngsters per show.

Frequently from two junior schools in our area we receive some nice letters containing praise and criticism of our work. The criticism is usually very shrewd. You cannot pass off rubbish to these little imps and get away with it. When we played *The Young Dick Whittington*, every one of these juniors who had seen the show wrote to point out that although the milestone to London pointed off right, Dick and his cat, Samantha, had gone off left.

One headmaster is such a sport and so understanding that when any of his pupils are in a show, he excuses them all homework for that week. They do it in their own time the next week, and they are excused should they be a little late in the mornings. He tells me that so sporting are the youngsters that very seldom is one of them late for school that week. Mutual understanding and trust are the secrets between teacher and pupil. When it happens it is one of the most beautiful things in this muddled, cacophonic world in which we live today.

A typical example of the apathy found within the teaching world, the sort of attitude I abhor, concerns the marvellous open-air theatre built at a school in Grimsby. It seats 1,000 to 1,500 and cost approximately £500, plus thousands of hours of loving labour on the part of its originator, Mr Colin Laycock, a teacher, and gangs of the much maligned teenagers. This theatre was opened on 23rd September 1959, by Dame Edith Evans, DBE.

I learn that after Mr Laycock left the school, the theatre has hardly been used. Would the sports masters have so neglected a sports stadium?

32

Summing Up

I have tried in the foregoing chapters to tell the plain facts: the story of the Stretford Children's Theatre. It has been my aim to describe what we do, how we do it, and perhaps most important, why we do it.

I feel, most emphatically, that in spite of all our frustrating difficulties, bitter disappointments and regretful financial losses the whole project has been, and is daily proving, immensely worth-while. I hope my words will have strengthened the converted, encouraged the faint-hearted, and stimulated those who have hitherto not been interested in children's theatre to think about it.

To those who refuse to listen, because they do not want their prejudices disturbed, I say nothing. If I said what I think about such people it would be too strong for publication, even in these days of four-letter words. That such people are a brake on progress is, of course, universally acknowledged.

Generally speaking, more people are interested in children's theatre than was the case twenty-one years ago when we founded our Theatre. Every year youth theatres of every kind are launched. Pockets of fierce, dynamic activity exist all over the country. This is exciting and magnificent. But time is appallingly short. Technological knowledge is progressing at an alarming rate. It is dazzling our younger generation with its icy, slick efficiency and precision. When we are in the presence of death, the sense and the appeal of life become heightened. So, as we see the massacre of all lovely things which is going on all around us, their value to the world becomes increasingly apparent to the thinking minority. We see the products of the pseudo-intelligentsia who unfortunately have commandeered the attention of the mass media.

> '. . . *wrecking what our age cannot replace*
> *To save its tasteless soul.*'

To our sensitive spirits this state of affairs is sheer agony.

Between the blind entry into this world, and the nebulous land which we enter at death and from which there is no certain return, we may choose, by means of free will, many ways of using the fleeting minute. Mechanization means that we are going to have increased leisure. What are we going to do with it?

We, in our Theatre, are actively busy in what is proving to be a pulsating revival through the ranks of our younger generation, and a renaissance of a passionate interest, but, what is even more thrilling and beneficial, a personal in-involvement in live theatre. I would like here to express an ardent wish, nay a strong plea.

The thought I know is in the heart of many pioneers in the field of youth drama, but perhaps because of a delicacy of spirit or an innate shyness, it is unspoken. This plea is that in all this feverish activity where we are experimenting and founding theatres of every type, we should not allow jealousies and rancour to creep in to mar our efforts. We are shouldering a great responsibility. Nothing should jeopardize our work. Earnest work of any kind should be encouraged, and it ill behoves any of us to belittle what someone else is doing, just because it does not happen to be to our personal liking.

Some of us have had to fight long and hard to get where we are. A little practical help, nay just an encouraging word at the right moment, instead of envy and carping would have made all the difference. For those who have had generous help, it would be noble to look upon the struggles of the zeal-ous with a kindly tolerance.

The simple Nativity Play, with Mary and Joseph dressed in curtains and the Wise Men wearing cardboard crowns, but presented with sincerity can mean as much to its audience as a play dressed by the Royal Shakespeare Theatre's wardrobe, and produced by Tyrone Guthrie means to a National Theatre assembly. To the five-year-old watching his friend playing Joseph, the impact may be beyond expression, as he watches, mouth open in sheer ecstasy. To sneer at it, as was done in one school of which I know, where a member of the staff was heard to remark that it was much ado about nothing, seems to me to be despicable.

It was a surprise to me recently to hear Mr Michael Croft telling the watching thousands on television that he was bringing his excellent Youth Theatre to Manchester, the main reason being because there was no youth theatre in the north.

At that very moment I was writing some notes that had been asked for by the press about our Theatre's twenty-first birthday then almost on us. I wondered what the Rhyl Children's Theatre, the Todmorden Children's Theatre, The Brighouse Children's Theatre and several other youth theatres in the north thought as they listened.

The idea that the northerner is a numbskull who has to await the arrival of the enlightened southerner in order to learn how to do things dies hard. The northerner often has the initiative to attack the project with bare hands and an empty coffer and by sheer grit and intelligence get the job done. I know I would have little hesitation in starting any project with the northern teenager.

I feel that thoughtless remarks can often build up an antagonistic atmosphere. This is a great pity. Any such movement is liable to dissipate much valuable energy in an unfriendly aura. We who believe in our work in youth theatre must get together in a co-operative spirit and learn what each group is doing. We must help each other in any way we can. Drama teachers must stick to their guns, and show reluctant head teachers and scornful colleagues that drama has a right to be considered side by side with other subjects on the curriculum.

Miss Jennie Lee, opening the British Children's Theatre Association's Conference, Easter, 1966, said she looked forward to the day when every Education Authority would have a Drama Adviser. At present a little more than one quarter of the 162 authorities in this country employ full-time drama advisers.

I maintain that a well organized children's theatre where children act is not harmful to the children. I have had twenty-one years' experience with our Theatre, and what we have done has been of inestimable benefit to our members.

A children's theatre is not an easy organization to run. It means hard work, disappointment and frustration. But what worth-while project does not? There will be mirages on the way, and opposition will loom large. Meet it with vital, positive plans. This means labour and sacrifice. A children's theatre of any kind requires a team to run it. We have always been short of adult helpers, but those we have had, have always been a marvellous, loyal team. And loyalty is what a director must have or his efforts are in vain.

We have had a long line, a pageant of colourful person-alities, who have enabled us to progress. They have helped in every capacity imaginable. In my memories I recall individuals and groups.

The Stretford Council, as a body, has valued our contribu-tion to the cultural life of the borough, and has shown its appreciation in a very practical way which I have mentioned in another section of this book.

Percy Lord, Chief Education Officer for the County of Lancashire, has on many occasions proved our very good friend. The interest of our genial and enlightened chief has always been of great moral assistance, in particular when things have looked very gloomy. His persistent and successful endeavours to obtain the lifeline of financial assistance when we were in dire need will ever remain a landmark in our history.

Of our Chairman, Alderman Harry Lord, and the late Mrs Lord I have already spoken. Harry, as he is affectionately thought of by us all, has ever been ready to help us in many valuable ways. Since 1950 he has never ceased to put in the necessary word, at local, county and national level. The word has always been lucid, and if necessary acid, but he has always been a power with which to be reckoned.

Then there is 'Blod', Miss Blodwyn Williams, our Business Manager, the only person who has been with me every foot of the way since 26th April 1945. She has laboured for us with a selfless devotion.

Following closely behind is Phyllis, Mrs Phyllis Buxton. It is to our deep regret that Phyllis cannot do much for us at the moment, as she has work which keeps her busy until late in the evening. For several years she was our Business Manager. Many were the times that Phyllis rushed straight from work to take over the Box Office and sacrificed her tea. Furthermore she was manager for the Top Five Rhythm Group when they were functioning. We all remember Phyllis with affection. Such loyalty as hers is priceless.

Our Catering Committee, Mrs Alice Hargreaves, Mrs Bullock and Mrs Fildes must have made thousands of cups of tea, both for our casts and audiences. They have saved my life many a time at dress rehearsals by quietly slipping into my hand the cup that cheers.

Mrs Veale, Betty to us, Mrs Walmsley and Miss Jones, who sit by the hour and iron and plan in the Wardrobe, are pearls beyond price.

A kaleidoscope of names and occasions flash through my mind. Colin, perspiring as he concreted the floor of the Coffee Bar, covered in soot and grime as he helped to clear the Headquarters when we bought it. Philip, Peter, Pat, Stuart, Shelagh, Sheila, Ann, Jennifer, Mary, in whose lap an affectionate cat gave birth to three kittens as she sat engrossed, watching June Ritchie rehearse a scene in *Romeo and Juliet*; Barbara and Alan Frost, joint secretaries; the late Mrs Taylor; my late comrades Bill Parkinson and Lorna; the late Ferney Leverett; the late Steven Browne, staunch friend and Stage Manager; pianists Hilda Bone, Lily Jones, Ida Scentlebury and Beryl Millward. I could go on for a long time. The line of devoted helpers stretches over twenty-two years.

To each and every one, mentioned and unmentioned, I offer my gratitude. No words could ever convey my real feeling. I look upon my young members as my family. Fate decreed I should never have a child of my own. My young artists have become my sons and daughters. No one could have a more fascinating brood. Rarely have they disappointed me.

Seldom is it given to a man to have a more understanding wife. The support she has given me over the years I have already related. It has never been stronger than at the present time. I am filled with gratitude.

There must be no lessening of effort in the days ahead. Rather must it be increased, particularly now we are aiming for that theatre. My war cry throughout this book has been that the arts must be saved at all costs. At the moment warmth seems to have gone from life. There remains only an unresponsive hardness. Because we have cluttered up life with man-made irrelevances, the core of warm expansive kindness has become encrusted with a shell of cynicism and pessimism. Only by a constant labour of honest endeavour can we, by means of the arts, thaw out life, as it seems, to life as it really is, rich, wonderful, ecstatic, rewarding. This enthusiastic endeavour does blossom, sometimes in the most unexpected places. It is sometimes apologetic. People have been too bashful to enthuse about it. If they have been bold enough to voice their zest, then the earthy, torpid boor has looked upon them as madmen.

How I long for more of these enthusiasts! I would rather dwell in restless argument with madmen of this calibre than I would live in brotherly deadliness with a husk of a human being whom the anaesthetizing thousands would call 'sane'.

Thank heaven there are signs of an awakening of an artistic

awareness. A handful of shining personalities like John English and Peter Slade are convincing some of the heavy eunuchs and acidulated vestals of the education world that this artistic passion is the glorious expression of *life*. It is not an escape from life, as the gross materialist would have it, but a glorious escape into life. The power which such an escape will generate will knock the emasculated, dreary existence which so many people endure into the middle of the next century, and inject a new meaning into this world.

The sparks are spluttering. Let us all supply the draught which will fan the raw material into one huge, glorious combustion of creative effort.

From questions I am asked by people I meet when I am lecturing about the Theatre, and particularly when I am adjudicating Youth Drama Festivals, I am well aware there are many individuals who are actively interested in children's theatre. Some of them have problems peculiar to their own situations. Others wish to know how to start a children's theatre, and are at a loss where to find help. Frequently people write to me. Others come to our headquarters and we have a private chat. I am always happy to be of service.

My publishers have most kindly agreed to co-operate with me in this endeavour. If you have any problem you would like to discuss or any point on which you think I might be able to help, please write to me, care of the publishers:

Faber and Faber Ltd,
24 Russell Square,
London, W.C.1.

Two things I ask. Do not expect a reply by return of post. I will answer as soon as I am able. As you will understand I am very busy, but I will answer all letters in strict rotation. The second request, please put in with your questions a stamped, addressed envelope.